# MY PRAYER BOOK

# MY PRAYER BOOK

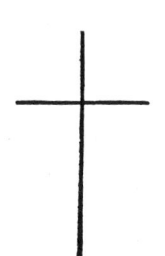

†

CONCORDIA PUBLISHING HOUSE
Saint Louis, Missouri

Copyright 1957
CONCORDIA PUBLISHING HOUSE
Saint Louis, Missouri
*Library of Congress Catalog Card No. 56-12420*
Eighth Printing 1967

MANUFACTURED IN THE UNITED STATES OF AMERICA

# *Preface*

"The effectual, fervent prayer of a righteous man" that "availeth much" is more than a striking sentence or a beautifully phrased paragraph. Faith in God, to whom we pray, is more important than the wording of the prayer. "Let him ask in faith, nothing wavering. For he that wavereth is like a wave of the sea driven with the wind and tossed. For let not that man think that he shall receive anything of the Lord" (James 1:6, 7). The wording of our prayer is of secondary importance. Indeed, Jesus once indicated that words are not even necessary for an acceptable prayer. "Your Father knoweth what things ye have need of, before ye ask Him" (Matthew 6:8).

Words, however, give expression to what is in our hearts. When, therefore, His disciples asked Jesus, "Lord, teach us to pray," the Master gave them the words of the model prayer, "The Lord's Prayer." Jesus Himself poured out His heart to His heavenly Father in words of a long prayer in the night in which He began His suffering for our redemption (John 17).

In adding MY PRAYER BOOK to the abundance of devotional and prayer books published in recent years, it is our hope not only to have provided acceptable, prepared prayers, but also to have offered suitable prayer patterns to aid those who do not seem to know how to give expression to what is in their hearts as they face the problems and temptations, the joys and sorrows, the successes and disappointments of life.

"Let us therefore come boldly unto the Throne of Grace, that we may obtain mercy and find grace to help in time of need" (Hebrews 4:16).

CONCORDIA PUBLISHING HOUSE

# Contents

|  | PAGE |
|---|---|
| *Preface* | vii |

## *Morning and Evening Prayers*

| First Week | 2 |
| Second Week | 15 |
| Third Week | 28 |
| Fourth Week | 41 |
| Additional Prayers | 54 |

## *Prayers for Christian Living*

| For More Abundant Living | 64 |
| For Purity of Heart | 65 |
| For Readiness to Forgive | 65 |
| For Finding Peace of Mind Through Forgiveness | 66 |
| For Finding Joy in My Forgiveness | 67 |
| For Overcoming My Worries | 68 |
| For Overcoming My Fears | 69 |
| For Overcoming My Doubts | 70 |
| For Overcoming My Disappointments | 71 |
| For Overcoming My Dissatisfaction | 72 |
| For Overcoming My Sensitiveness | 73 |
| For Overcoming My Self-Pity | 74 |
| For Overcoming My Intolerance | 75 |
| For Relief from Frustration | 76 |
| For Grace to Adjust Myself | 77 |
| For the Grace of Humility | 78 |
| For Grace to Be Patient | 79 |
| For the Grace of a Consecrated Life | 80 |
| For the Grace to Be True to Myself | 81 |
| For the Grace to Make the Right Decisions | 82 |

| | |
|---|---|
| Gratitude for the Blessings Received | 83 |
| Gratitude for Special Blessings Received | 84 |
| Gratitude for the Joy of Being a Christian | 85 |
| For Conquering Alcoholism | 86 |

## *Prayers for Christian Worship*

| | |
|---|---|
| For the Joy of Worship | 88 |
| Before Going to Church | 89 |
| After Attending Church | 89 |
| For Baptismal Grace | 90 |
| For My Communion Sunday | 91 |
| For Bible Sunday | 92 |
| For a Better Understanding of My Bible | 93 |
| On Joining the Church | 94 |
| Taking an Office in the Congregation | 94 |
| For New Year's Day | 95 |
| For the Epiphany of Our Lord | 96 |
| For the Lenten Season | 97 |
| For Palm Sunday | 98 |
| For Good Friday | 99 |
| My Easter Prayer | 100 |
| The Ascension of Our Lord | 102 |
| For Pentecost Sunday | 103 |
| For Trinity Sunday | 104 |
| For Mother's Day | 105 |
| For Father's Day | 106 |
| For Reformation Day | 107 |
| For Thanksgiving Day | 108 |
| For Christmas Eve | 109 |
| For Christmas Day | 110 |
| For New Year's Eve | 111 |
| For the Pastor | 112 |
| For the Congregation | 112 |
| For the Sunday School and Its Classes | 113 |
| On Opening of School Term | 114 |
| By the Teachers of the Church | 115 |
| By the Youth of the Church | 116 |
| By the Youth Workers | 117 |
| By Camp Workers | 118 |
| For the Missions in Foreign Fields | 119 |
| For Missions at Home | 120 |

| | |
|---|---|
| For Missionary Zeal | 121 |
| For the Spread of the Gospel by Radio and Television | 122 |
| For Ability to Witness | 123 |
| For the Unconverted | 124 |
| For a Specific Person to Whom One Desires to Witness | 125 |
| For the Spiritual Welfare of Friends, Relatives, and Fellow Workers | 126 |
| For Opportunities for Kingdom Service | 127 |

## Prayers for the Family Life

| | |
|---|---|
| My Birthday | 130 |
| Upon My Graduation | 131 |
| For a Life Companion | 132 |
| For One Disappointed in Love | 132 |
| On the Day of Betrothal | 133 |
| On Expecting a Baby | 135 |
| On the Coming of the Baby (Mother's Prayer) | 136 |
| For My Wedding Anniversary | 137 |
| For God-fearing Children | 138 |
| Thanks for Godly Children | 139 |
| For a High School Son or Daughter | 140 |
| For a College Student Away from Home | 141 |
| Of Parents for a Mentally Retarded Child | 142 |
| Of Parents for a Physically Handicapped Child | 143 |
| Of Parents for Son or Daughter Who Has Strayed | 144 |
| In Marital Difficulties | 145 |
| For One Absent from the Family | 146 |
| For the Families of Those in Service | 146 |
| For My Family While I Am in Service | 147 |
| For One of the Family in Service | 148 |
| Family Reunion | 149 |
| For Travel by Land, Sea, or Air | 150 |
| For Families Having Misunderstandings | 151 |
| For the Lonely | 155 |
| For Parents | 156 |
| For Children | 158 |

xi

## Prayers for Various Occupations

| | |
|---|---|
| Before Going to Work | 160 |
| On Returning from Work | 161 |
| On Taking a New Position | 162 |
| On Receiving a Promotion | 164 |
| When Going on Vacation | 165 |
| On Returning from Vacation | 165 |
| While on Strike | 166 |
| For the Unemployed | 167 |
| The Businessman | 168 |
| The Laboring Man | 169 |
| Labor Leaders | 170 |
| Management | 171 |
| For Guidance in Vocation | 172 |
| For Guidance in the Choice of a Vocation | 173 |
| Doctors | 174 |
| Nurses | 175 |
| Workers in Hospitals and Nursing Homes | 176 |
| Lawyers | 177 |
| State Officials | 178 |
| City Officials | 179 |
| Teachers | 179 |
| Technicians | 181 |
| Scientists | 182 |
| Farmers | 183 |
| Of a Handicapped Child of God | 184 |

## Prayers Pertaining to National and International Life

| | |
|---|---|
| For Peace | 188 |
| For Government | 189 |
| For the President of the United States | 190 |
| For the Nation | 191 |
| For the City | 192 |
| For Friendship Among the Nations | 193 |
| For Better Understanding Among the Nations | 194 |

| | |
|---|---|
| For Washington's Birthday | 194 |
| For Memorial Day | 195 |
| For Dominion Day | 197 |
| For Independence Day | 198 |
| For Labor Day | 199 |
| For Veterans' Day | 200 |
| For the Opening of Congress | 201 |
| During Wartime | 201 |
| By Men and Women in the Armed Services | 202 |
| During Unfavorable Weather | 203 |
| For Rain | 204 |
| In Days of Drought | 205 |

## Prayers in Time of Sickness

| | |
|---|---|
| Before an Operation | 208 |
| After an Operation | 209 |
| Prayers for the Sickroom | 209 |
| Prayers During the Convalescent Period | 218 |
| At the Approach of Death | 222 |
| After a Death in the Family | 223 |
| For the Sorrowing | 224 |
| Intercessions for the Sick | 225 |

## Table Prayers

| | |
|---|---|
| Grace at Meals | 228 |
| Prayers of Thanks | 229 |

## The Benedictions of the Lord

| | |
|---|---|
| The Old Testament Benediction | 234 |
| The New Testament Benedictions | 234 |

| | |
|---|---|
| *Where to Find It in the Bible* | 237 |
| *Outstanding Stories in the Bible* | 238 |
| *Outstanding Chapters of the Old Testament* | 238 |
| *Outstanding Chapters of the New Testament* | 239 |

*Morning and Evening Prayers*

## THE FIRST WEEK

*Sunday Morning*

Eternal and everlasting Father, in whose presence I pass my fleeting years, upheld by Thy grace and power, make Thy love real to me as I worship Thee this day. Grant that Thy Holy Spirit may strengthen my faith and my resolve to serve Thee with greater faithfulness. May nothing be more precious to me than the Gospel of the redeeming love of Thy Son, Jesus, my Savior.

Create in me a clean heart. Remove all distracting thoughts from my mind as I come into Thy presence to hear Thy Word and make my prayers and my confession of faith to Thee. May I deeply appreciate the great love of Thy Son, who went to Calvary to pay for my many sins with His own lifeblood. Forgive me daily. May the suffering of my Savior and His pain on the cross open my eyes to the marvels of His love and the greatness of my sin. Fill my heart with peace and the joy of forgiveness.

Accomplish Thy will in me. Strengthen my resolution to serve Thee more faithfully. Help me to overcome all sluggishness to worship Thee and all indifference to Thy Word. Let me conquer my fears and my self-pitying moods. On this day of worship let me sing praises to Thee. Help me to dedicate myself again to Thy Son Jesus Christ, who rose from the dead and lives forevermore. Amen.

*Sunday Evening*

As this day comes to a close, I gratefully acknowledge Thy goodness and mercy, O Lord, in granting to me the privilege of hearing Thy Word, the glorious Gospel of my salvation. Thy promises enable me to look upward with confidence and forward with courage. Bless Thou the labors of my hands, give me to understand my duties and tasks. Enrich my week with blessings from Thy bountiful hands. Grant me the grace to live daily in Thy presence, doing the things pleasing to Thee and helpful to my companions on the way.

Deepen my love for Thee. Keep me faithful to Thy Word, and help me to reduce to practice the directives given me today. Forgive me all my sins, especially every indifference of heart toward Thy Gospel. Bless me this night, and protect all Thy children. Bless my family, my friends, my pastor, and my church. Bless my co-workers throughout this week with Thy gracious benedictions. In Jesus' name I ask this. Amen.

*Monday Morning*

Gracious God, heavenly Father, I thank Thee for Thy mercy, which has kept me from all harm and danger in the darkness of the night now past. Banish also the darkness of sin from my life by Thy forgiveness, for Jesus my Savior's sake.

Let me begin the duties of my calling today with the assurance that Thou wilt look with favor on the work of my hands. Prosper whatever I do that my earnings may be sufficient for my needs and the wants of those whom Thou hast committed to my care. Teach me to give cheerfully of my earnings to the support of Thy church and the relief of the poor and needy. Help me to remember today the admonition of my Savior: "Seek ye first the kingdom of God and His righteousness, and all these things shall be added unto you." In that spirit let me begin the tasks of this day. Amen.


*Monday Evening*

O God of love and grace, in this evening hour I humbly pray Thee to forgive me for Jesus' sake all that was wrong in my life today.

I confess that at times I find myself doing what I do not want to do, and sometimes not doing what I know I should do. Have mercy on me! Send Thy Holy Spirit into my heart that I may grow in grace and in the knowledge of Jesus Christ, my Savior. Help me to abound in those things which are well-pleasing in Thy sight.

I thank Thee for the good health with which Thou hast blessed me so that I can do the work of my calling. Remember all who are distressed by sickness and sorrow, and apply to their wounded hearts the healing balm of Thy precious promises.

Let peaceful sleep close my eyes tonight, and, if it be Thy will, awaken me on the morrow refreshed in body and soul. And when my last night on this earth has come, grant me to see the more perfect day in glory everlasting. For Jesus' sake. Amen.

*Tuesday Morning*

Heavenly Father, Thy will be done on earth as it is in heaven. Grant that Thy will may be done in the hearts and the lives of people everywhere, and grant me the grace to be ever aware of Thy will and to submit to Thee in all things. Give me faithfulness in my work, and crown my labors with Thy blessing.

Restrain the rulers of the earth who place their own will above Thine and who thereby cause suffering and heartache among their people. Help them to see that peace and good order can prevail only as long as Thy will is done.

Convince all ministers of the Gospel that Thy will is done when they preach and teach Thy Word in truth, when they admonish the erring and comfort the sorrowing, and when they point their hearers to Christ and Thee.

Keep me and all Christians mindful of Thy commandments and of our duty to serve Thee. Above all, give us a burning love for souls and a sense of urgency in proclaiming the free salvation which Thou hast made ours through Jesus Christ.

May I trust in Thy promises and ask no more than Thou hast promised. In prosperity keep me humble; in adversity keep me strong; and at all times give me a deep devotion to duty and confident trust in Thy mercy, through our Lord and Savior Jesus Christ. Amen.

*Tuesday Evening*

Dear Father in heaven, I thank Thee for Thy care and protection, for the health and strength necessary for the work of this day, and for the answer to my prayers and the prayers of Christians everywhere.

Be with me also this night, and keep all harm and danger from me. Forgive my sins, and assure me of Thy abiding grace and mercy. Keep all who are near and dear to me in Thy watchful care. Give me a quiet, restful sleep, and thereby prepare me for the tasks of another day.

Cleanse my heart from all thoughts of hate or envy, and help me to live peaceably with all people. Make me helpful, kind, and considerate that I may live my life for Thee and for others.

May thoughts of Thee be in my heart when I fall asleep and when I awake. If this night should be my last on earth, may I fall asleep in Jesus and awake in Thy presence. Amen.


*Wednesday Morning*

Lord Jesus, who art my everliving and everloving Savior, I thank Thee that Thou dost neither slumber nor sleep and that Thou hast protected me by Thy mighty hand through the night.

Open my eyes to see the blessings which Thou hast prepared for me this day. For the love of friends which will enrich this day, I thank Thee. For the ability to work and to serve others, I praise Thee. For the gifts to be granted me this day, I honor Thee.

Keep me firm in faith, watchful in temptation, humble in my successes, and joyful in the face of afflictions, for Thy name's sake. Without Thee

I can do nothing, but I can do all things through Thee, who strengthenest me.

Help me this day to bear clear witness to the hope begotten in me by Thy resurrection from the dead. Grant me Thy Holy Spirit that I may be dead to sin and alive to holiness. Use me this day to bring Thy Gospel to some persons who are as sheep without a shepherd, so that they may learn to know Thee, the Good Shepherd, and find in Thee rest and peace for their souls.

Lead me in the paths of righteousness this day, Lord Jesus, for Thy name's sake. Amen.

*Wednesday Evening*

At the end of another day, dear heavenly Father, I praise Thee for Thy goodness and adore Thee for Thy mercy. Thou hast not left me nor forsaken me, even as Thou didst promise. But I have failed Thee and forsaken Thee by sinning, and I ask Thee, for the sake of Thy Son and my Redeemer, to cleanse me from all my sins.

From the rising of the sun to the shadows of this night Thou hast been with me to bless, help, guide, strengthen, and comfort me. I am not worthy of the least of all the mercies and of all the truth which Thou hast shown to me, Thy servant. I thank Thee, Father.

I ask Thee to look with tender pity upon all who are without the comfort of Thy Gospel. Turn their hearts in repentant faith toward Thy Son, and cause Thy Gospel of forgiveness to be proclaimed to all who have not yet heard of Thy great grace in Christ Jesus.

Grant me sound rest this night that I may arise refreshed and in good health on the morrow, ready to serve Thee in cheerful obedience to Thy good and gracious will. Speak peace to my soul, for in Thee do I hope. Amen.

*Thursday Morning*

> *Another day is dawning;*
> *Dear Master, let it be*
> *On earth or else in heaven*
> *Another day for Thee.*

Gracious Father in heaven, I know not when Thou wilt call me home — for in the midst of life we are in death. Regardless of the number of my days on earth, cause me always to be prepared to answer Thy summons. I know that the road of my life leads finally to Thy heavenly mansions above. Equip me for the trials and pitfalls that beset my way through life, and teach me to perform in Thy holy name each duty which confronts me. Remind me daily that I am a pilgrim without a continuing city here, and help me to assist my fellow travelers by sharing their burdens and showing them the glory of the life in Thee.

Whether my pathway leads to hilltops fair and high or through the sunless valleys where the shadows lie, it matters little, for I know that Thou art with me and that underneath are Thy everlasting arms. Where Thou dost lead me I shall gladly go. Oh, guide me unerringly on life's uncertain way here to my heavenly homeland there. In Jesus' name. Amen.

*Thursday Evening*

As this day closes, dear heavenly Father, I come to Thee to thank Thee for Thy unfailing love, which even during the darkness of night continues to shine upon me and those whom I love. The wrongs and mistakes that have marred my life again today show me plainly how much I need Thee in my everyday life. Pardon me for Jesus' sake, and take away every impure thought and wish. Make my heart right, and make my actions reflect Thy love. I want to become more like Jesus, Thy dear Son, who went about doing good. Heal the sick, relieve the suffering, strengthen the weak, recall the erring, curb the wicked, help the troubled, comfort the sorrowing, and give peace to the dying. O Thou who dost not sleep, keep me safe until morning comes again. In Jesus' name. Amen.

*Friday Morning*

Almighty God and Father, the light of day summons me to the duties and privileges of the stewardship of life. Help me to be a good steward by revealing to me Thy will for my life. May I make the best possible use of the talents which Thou hast given me, so that I may always be ready to give an account of my stewardship.

In the activities of this day give me the wisdom to recognize whatever is evil before I am ensnared by it. Grant me the strength to resist every temptation to sin and shame. Let me never be afraid to say, "How can I do this great wickedness and sin against God?"

Grant me the opportunity today to do good to someone who is in need of my love. When others deny Thee, give me the courage to confess my faith. Show me how to live in a manner worthy of Thy holy name.

In Jesus' name I pray. Amen.

*Friday Evening*

O Lord God, I thank Thee that the knowledge of Thy presence kept me from gross sin today, made me more gracious in dealing with my fellow men and more zealous in performing the duties of my calling.

O Lord,

*I need Thy presence every passing hour;
What but Thy grace can foil the Tempter's power?
Who like Thyself my guide and stay can be?
Through cloud and sunshine, oh, abide with me!*

I pray, heavenly Father, that Thou wouldst reveal Thyself especially to those tonight who are passing through trial and tribulation. Teach them to know that "ills have no weight and tears no bitterness, with Thee at hand to bless," and that "nothing shall be able to separate us from the love of God which is in Christ Jesus, our Lord."

Abide with me in the coming night, and let me hear Thee say to me: "Fear thou not, for I am with thee; be not dismayed, for I am thy God. I will strengthen thee; yea, I will help thee; yea, I will uphold thee with the right hand of My righteousness." Amen.

*Saturday Morning*

"O Lord, Thou hast searched me and known me. Thou knowest my downsitting and mine uprising. Thou understandest my thoughts afar off. There is not a word in my tongue, but, lo, O Lord, Thou knowest it altogether."

As I begin a new day with Thee, search my heart, dear Lord, and purify my affections so that I may love only those things which please Thee, and put Thee first in everything.

Help me to overcome the temptations I will meet this day. Strengthen my faith that victory over the devil may be mine to Thy glory. Keep me mindful of the sufficiency of Thy grace, and let Thy strength be made perfect in my weakness.

Give me the grace to guard against sins of the tongue, and preserve me from thinking evil in my heart against my neighbor. Teach me the joy of walking the ways of Thy commandments, and bless those who walk in Thy fear and favor.

Watch over me this day when dangers overtake me, and ward off any evil of body or soul. If afflictions are to come to me this day by Thy gracious direction, keep me humble and obedient to Thy loving will.

Thanks be to Thee, Lord God, for all Thy past benefits and for Thy promises of future mercies. Direct my day in such a way that I may learn to praise Thee better tonight for the favors of this day. Amen.

*Saturday Evening*

Lord Jesus Christ, Thou Author and Finisher of my faith, I thank Thee for having brought me safely to the end of another week of my earthly pilgrimage to heaven. Praise and thanks be to Thee for having earned a perfect salvation for me, for bringing me to faith in Thee through the Gospel, and for having kept me in the true faith to this moment. Keep me in my baptismal grace so that I may, at the end of my pilgrimage, rejoice with all Thy saints over the wonders of Thy eternal love.

For the blessings of this past week I thank Thee, dear Lord, and pray Thee for Thy mercies' sake to continue to deal graciously with me. Grant Thy pardon for the sins by which I have offended Thee and hurt my neighbor.

Help me to look forward eagerly to the privilege of entering Thy house of worship on the morrow. Grant me the grace to believe what I shall hear from Thy Word, and give me the joy of offering to Thee the sacrifices of my praise.

Lord, Thou hast opened mine eyes to the beauty of Thy grace. Close my eyes in rest, and let me see in the morning the sunshine of Thy favor and the brightness of Thy glory. Amen.

## THE SECOND WEEK

*Sunday Morning*

Lord God, Father, Son, and Holy Spirit, grant Thy sanctifying presence as I join my fellow Christians on this day in worshiping Thee in the beauty of holiness. "Lord, I have loved the habitation of Thy house and the place where Thine honor dwelleth." "How amiable are Thy tabernacles, O Lord of hosts! My soul longeth, yea, even fainteth, for the courts of the Lord; my heart and flesh crieth out for the living God!" "A day in Thy courts is better than a thousand. I had rather be a doorkeeper in the house of my God than to dwell in the tents of wickedness."

Bless the preaching of Thy Word in all the world today that many people of all races and nations may be brought to repentance and faith in Jesus Christ.

Bless my hearing of Thy Word today that I may be confirmed in my faith and strengthened in my consecration to serve Thee. Keep me aware that I must be a doer of the Word and not a hearer only, lest I deceive myself.

All glory, praise, and honor be to Thee, the Father, the Son, and the Holy Ghost, ever one God, world without end. Amen.

*Sunday Evening*

Heavenly Father, at the close of another day dedicated to Thee, I come before Thee with my evening sacrifice of prayer and praise.

I pray Thee that the blessings of this day, hearing Thy Word, singing Thy praise, feeling Thy presence, enjoying the fellowship of Christian people, may go with me in the week that lies ahead. Like this day of rest, so let also the days of toil be consecrated to Thee.

I praise Thee for Thy mercy and grace in Jesus Christ and for all the evidences that Thou dost draw me ever closer to Thee with lovingkindness. I can never repay Thee for all that Thou hast done for me. Accept, I pray Thee, the praise of my lips and the dedication of my life.

For the coming night I commit myself into Thy hands; let Thy holy angels be with me that the wicked Foe may have no power over me. Amen.

*Monday Morning*

Dear heavenly Father, I thank Thee for having kept me safe during the night. Now I pause at the gateway of another week to ask Thee to go with me. I do not know what this week holds in store — pleasure or pain, health or sickness, sunshine or shadow. However, I am not afraid if Thou wilt be my Companion, for Thou dost love me with an everlasting love and dost guard and protect me from all evil. I need Thy presence every step of the way. At the beginning of this week I ask only that Thou wouldst stay close beside me, for, though I know not what the future holds, I know who holds the future. Bless me in whatever I do. Make me strong physically, mentally, morally, and spiritually. Watch over me and over those whom I love. I ask this in the name of Thy beloved Son, my Savior and Redeemer. Amen.

*Monday Evening*

As evening comes, I thank Thee, dear heavenly Father, who didst create day and night, for the health and protection Thou hast given me this day. I do not deserve even the least of Thy many blessings. For Jesus' sake forgive my sins and shortcomings, particularly if I have offended some soul weak in faith or if I have neglected the opportunity to lead someone to Thee. Grant me Thy Spirit's power so that each day I may grow in faith and in the knowledge of my Savior.

Guard my home. Protect my family. Bless the friends I love. Look with mercy upon all people. Comfort those who have experienced sorrow. Cause the Gospel of Thy love in Christ to stir men's hearts. Grant me and all men a greater appreciation of Thy mercy so that we may serve Thee more joyfully and eagerly. Be with me always. And now grant me a restful sleep; for Jesus' sake. Amen.

*Tuesday Morning*

Lord God, my heavenly Father, at the beginning of this new day I ask Thee for the gift of Thy Holy Spirit and the gift of a new spirit. As Thou hast granted me protection from all danger in this night now past, be merciful to me and continue through the day to guard and keep me from every evil of body and soul, property and honor.

Open my eyes to every opportunity to do good, for Thou hast created me in Christ Jesus unto good works and hast foreordained that I should walk in them. Give me faithfulness for every task set before me, and grant me grace to render service to all men as unto Thee, my Lord.

Help me to live this day as though Jesus died yesterday, arose today, and were coming back tomorrow. Let His Cross be my glory and His favor my crown. Let His return to Judgment not frighten me but stimulate me to earnest attention to my faith and to faithfulness to Him.

Grant me enough success today to be encouraged and enough difficulties to be humbled. Give me strength to overcome when I am tempted to do wrong and to seize my opportunities to do good.

> *Guide me, O Thou great Jehovah,*
> *Pilgrim through this barren land.*
> *I am weak, but Thou art mighty;*
> *Hold me with Thy powerful hand.*
> *Amen.*

*Tuesday Evening*

Lord Jesus, who dost welcome all who come to Thee in a humble and contrite spirit, I lay before Thee the burden of my sins and ask Thee for Thy gracious pardon. I have not done this day what was my duty to do, and I confess my sins to Thee, who alone canst cover my transgressions, and I pray Thee to remember them no more.

Help me to be stronger because of Thy forgiveness, happier because of Thy mercy, and more willing to serve Thee because of Thy love.

Watch over me this night, and favor me with refreshing rest and peaceful sleep. Should I close my eyes in sleep for the last time this night, awaken me to the brightness of Thy glory and to the bliss of eternal fellowship with Thee.

Thou hast been my Refuge and Strength, a very present Help in trouble. Thou hast been my Shield and exceeding great Reward. How can I thank Thee for Thy kindness, and how can I praise Thee sufficiently for Thy mercies? Eternity will be too short, Lord Jesus, to utter all Thy praise.

I commend myself, my body and soul, into Thy safekeeping. Thou art faithful, and in Thee do I trust. Amen.

*Wednesday Morning*

Unto Thee, O Lord, do I lift up my heart in this morning hour, sincerely grateful for the opportunities of another day. Bless me in what I do today that all may be acceptable to Thee. Grant me such success in my work as Thou knowest to be best for me. Keep me always mindful that all depends on my possessing Thine abundant grace and blessing.

Help me, I pray, to reflect in my life the infinite love with which Thou didst love me in Jesus Christ, my Savior. In all my dealings with my fellow men help me to love them as I love myself, and to do for them what I would have them do for me.

Make me strong to resist any temptation to take what does not rightfully belong to me. Give me the courage to suffer losses rather than to inflict them on others. Help me to realize that life consists not in the abundance of things which

I possess, but rather in what I do with what I possess, whether much or little. Teach me to know that godliness with contentment is great gain and to live accordingly.

In Jesus' name I pray, and in His name I begin the tasks of this day. Amen.

*Wednesday Evening*

Heavenly Father, I thank Thee for the privilege of speaking to Thee in prayer. It is good to know that I may come to Thee, the almighty Creator of all things in heaven and on earth, as my heavenly Father for Jesus' sake. Give me the faith of a loving child, never doubting that Thou wilt always hear my prayer. If sometimes Thou dost not answer my prayers exactly as I have asked, then let me have the childlike trust to believe that Thou, heavenly Father, knowest best what to give me and what to withhold.

I thank Thee that Thou didst send Thine only-begotten Son into the world to redeem also me from sin and death. Help me to live as a child of Thine, avoiding sin and serving Thee with a consecrated life.

Take into Thy special care tonight all those who are heavy-laden with cares and crosses. Watch with the sick; comfort those who mourn the loss of a loved one. Reveal Thyself to them as the heavenly Father to whom they may always go in the day of trouble.

And now let me find rest and peace in refreshing sleep. In Jesus' name. Amen.

*Thursday Morning*

Dear heavenly Father, forgive my sins and help me, in gratitude to Thee, to forgive those who sin against me.

O Lord, my heart is by nature proud and unforgiving. It is hard for me to confess my sins, even to Thee. Help me to see clearly that I offend Thee daily and that, indeed, I deserve nothing but punishment. Help me to acknowledge freely that I am worthy of none of the things for which I pray, and help me to say with the Publican: "God, be merciful to me, a sinner."

My own struggles to be obedient to Thee remind me that my fellow men have similar struggles. Give them all believing hearts and help them in serving Thee. When they sin, make me as charitable toward them as Thou art charitable toward me, and help them find their way back to Thee. When they sin against me, give me an understanding and a forgiving heart. Make me willing to forgive because Thou hast loved me and forgiven me so much. When I sin against them, move them to forgive me, that together we may walk the way of life; for Jesus' sake. Amen.

*Thursday Evening*

Lord and Savior Jesus Christ, tonight I bring the needs of the church before Thee. I thank Thee for all Christian churches and schools, for the teaching of the Gospel far and near, and for the messengers of peace who carry Thy Word to mansions and cottages, to children and to higher schools of learning, to people of all races far and near, to rich and poor alike.

Fire every member of Thy church with Thy Holy Spirit, Lord Jesus, that all may speak the things which they have experienced in their hearts. Help us to proclaim Thy love for sinful man and the joyous faith that Thou art our God and Savior. Make eager witnesses of all believers, and give also me the grace to speak Thy Word as occasion offers.

Grant me Thy grace that some soul may learn the way of life from me, that together we may rejoice with Thee in all eternity. Help me especially to witness among my relatives and friends and among the members of my own family.

And now, grant peaceful rest, and renew my body and spirit for the duties of tomorrow. In rest and at work, gracious Lord, be at my side to strengthen, to guide, and to bless. Amen.

*Friday Morning*

Gracious Lord and adorable Savior, in this morning hour I praise Thee who hast redeemed me through Thy sacrifice on Calvary. Thereby Thou hast purchased me to be Thine own. Grant that I may serve Thee with willing heart and untiring devotion to show my appreciation of Thy great love for me. Make me an instrument of consecrated service to Thee that all I do today will give glory to Thy holy name. Help me by Thy grace and through strength coming from Thee to resist every temptation to sin; let me not deny Thy name nor ever be ashamed of Thee. Enrich this day with a genuine Christian joy and a sincere appreciation of Thy goodness and Thy peace, which fills the heart and mind through faith in Thy redeeming Cross. Wherever an encouraging word is needed, let me give it. Whenever a helping hand is needed to lift a burden, make mine ready, and guide my footsteps into those ways that are pleasing to Thee. May my whole day be dedicated to Thee, who art my Savior and my Shepherd. Amen.


*Friday Evening*

Lord, with grateful heart I come into Thy presence in this evening hour, mindful of Thy many mercies which have enriched my day. Thou hast forgiven me all my sins, comforted me in my disappointments, calmed me when irritated, and strengthened me in the face of temptations and doubt.

I praise Thee, Lord of heaven and earth, for Thy goodness and Thy grace. Grant that I be faithful to Thee as Thou hast been to me. Thou hast poured out upon me blessing after blessing and hast brought peace to my soul through the many promises of Thy Gospel. Draw me closer to Thyself with Thy forgiving love. Bring to my heart that peace which has been purchased for me on Calvary through Thy Son, Jesus Christ, my Lord. Remove from my evening hours all worry and fear, that I may sleep under Thy watchful care, knowing that all is well because Thou art with me. And when the morning comes, let Thy presence guide me through the day, mindful at all times that Jesus Christ is my Shepherd and Friend. Amen.


*Saturday Morning*

Lord Jesus Christ, Thou Sun of Righteousness, shine into my heart and life today. Help me to reflect Thy light that someone who does not yet know Thee as Lord and Savior may be directed to Thee.

I thank Thee that Thou hast borne the guilt of my sins. Let the sin and evil that may threaten today have no power over me. Grant me the grace to recognize Thy will and the faith to do it. In all my dealings with others today, let me be guided by Thy precept: "Whatsoever ye would that men should do to you, do ye even so to them."

Keep me united with Thee, as a branch of the true Vine, that I may draw from Thee the strength to abound in good works. Mayest Thou be glorified today in all that I do; for Thy name's sake. Amen.

*Saturday Evening*

At the close of another week, O gracious God, I thank Thee that Thou hast kept me from harm and danger of body and soul. I am grateful, too, that Thou hast blessed the labors of my hands. I am not worthy of all the goodness and of all the mercies which I have enjoyed in the past. Continue to bless me in body and soul with whatever is for my good.

In the quiet of this evening hour I would prepare my heart to worship Thee on the morrow in spirit and in truth. Bless the preaching of the Gospel in all the world that Thy Word may accomplish what Thou dost desire, even the saving of souls bought by the precious blood of Jesus Christ.

Send Thy Holy Spirit also on the congregation where I intend to worship tomorrow. May the hearing of Thy Word serve to strengthen my faith in Thee, the one true God, Father, Son, and Holy Ghost, and inspire me to holiness of living.

With the knowledge that Thou, heavenly Father, dost love me, I retire tonight safe in Thy care and keeping. Amen.

## THE THIRD WEEK

*Sunday Morning*

Lord God, merciful Father, I praise Thee for the light of this day, when by Thy Spirit Thou wilt shine in my heart through the preaching and teaching of Thy Gospel. Open my eyes that I may behold the wondrous truths of Thy salvation and find new strength and hope in Thy promises.

Bless the preaching and teaching of Thy Word throughout Thy church, and cause Thy Gospel to fall as good seed upon good ground that it may bear abundant fruit. Give power and conviction to Thy ministers that their testimony to Thy holiness and grace may ring clear and true to Thy revealed Word.

Keep me from mere formality in my worship, from praying with the lips only while the heart is far from Thee, from failure to listen to the sermon with eager expectation as a message from Thee. Grant me the grace to bring my burdens to church and to leave them there at Thy feet.

Guide Thy wandering children into Thy house this day so that they may find true adventure in the abundant life which Thou hast promised all who love Thee.

"Let the words of my mouth and the meditation of my heart be acceptable in Thy sight, O Lord, my Strength and my Redeemer." Amen.

*Sunday Evening*

Lord Jesus, by Thy grace I have this day accepted Thy invitation: "Come unto Me, all ye that labor and are heavy-laden, and I will give you rest." I thank Thee that by Thy obedient life and innocent death upon the cross Thou hast removed the crushing burden of my sins. I praise Thee for the peace of mind and heart which Thou didst bestow by Thy promises of unfailing help and strength. I bless Thee for having made known once more the paths I am to walk in following after Thee.

Bless all those who made this day of worship meaningful and rewarding for me: my pastor, my Sunday school teacher, the organist, the choir, and my fellow Christians who gave me the benefit of their fellowship and prayers.

Help me this week to live Thy Word. Bless the offerings I have brought for the extension of Thy kingdom. By Thy Spirit comfort those who could not for valid reasons be in God's house today.

"Lord, I have loved the habitation of Thy house and the place where Thine honor dwelleth!" Amen.

*Monday Morning*

At the beginning of another week of work I ask Thee, good Lord, to remember me in Thy mercy and to look with favor upon my activities.

Help me to be a better Christian this week. Strengthen my faith, increase my hope, and nourish my love to Thee and to all men.

Preserve me from pride, for Thou dost resist the proud and givest grace only to the humble. Teach me to cast all my cares upon Thee, for Thou hast promised to care for me. Keep me from the love of money, lest I err from the faith and pierce myself through with many sorrows. Watch over me in moments of danger and temptation, and help me to do justly, to love mercy, and to walk humbly with Thee, my God.

I thank Thee for the opportunities to be a blessing to others and to be blessed by Thee this week. Let me rejoice at every chance to do good, and let me bear with patient forgiveness any evil done to me.

Give me not tasks equal to my strength, but strength equal to my tasks. Grant me the grace to live this day as though it were my last on earth and the first with Thee in heaven. Hear me for the sake of Jesus Christ, Thy Son, my Lord. Amen.

*Monday Evening*

O Father of mercies and God of all comfort, thanks be to Thee for having dealt graciously with me this day. I have sinned against Thee, but Thou hast not forsaken me. Forgive me and cleanse me with the blood of Thy Son.

Grant me a refreshing night of rest and sleep, and permit me to rise in the morning, ready to live another day to Thy glory.

Watch over my loved ones near at hand and far away, refresh them with rest, and protect them with Thy mighty hand.

As I have come another day closer to eternity, keep me in the true faith in Thy Son as my only Redeemer from sin. Direct my thoughts and aims heavenward, lest I become too attached to the vanities of this life. Give me a sense of balance to enable me to rejoice in my earthly blessings without losing interest in my heavenly crown.

Look with mercy on those who this night are lonely, hungry, ill-clothed, or despondent. Give me compassion to pity them and to help them in their need. Turn their hearts in faith to the

Cross of Thy Son, and give them pardon and hope. Make me thankful for my security in Thee, and let me be Thy instrument in showing mercy to the needy. Amen.

*Tuesday Morning*

Gracious and holy God, I thank Thee for Thy mercies which are new to me each morning. I am not worthy of Thy many blessings and Thy great love toward me. Often I have offended Thee. I ask Thee not to hold my sins against me, but to blot them out with the blood of Thy beloved Son, who died also for me. Help me to live more and more according to Thy will. Make my thoughts charitable, my words kind, and my deeds selfless. Let my light shine before men that I may glorify Thee and draw others to Thy kingdom. Make me ever humble and willing in Thy service.

*Oh, help me, Lord, this day to be
Thine own dear child — to follow Thee.
  Amen.*

*Tuesday Evening*

Again today Thou hast blessed me, dear Lord, above all that I could ask or think. Accept my heartfelt thanks for Thy loving care and Thy undeserved mercies. Thou hast permitted me to perform my tasks safe from harm and evil and hast filled my life with Thy generous bounties. Bless Thy children everywhere. Comfort and help all those who look to Thee in need. Enlarge Thy kingdom, and grant me grace always to confess Christ by word and deed. Pardon my sins, and let nothing come between Thee and me. Direct Thy holy angels to watch over me and my loved ones wherever they may be. With the close of this day of grace, give me restful sleep so that I may awaken tomorrow refreshed and strengthened to meet the cares and problems, the tasks and opportunities, of another day. This I ask in Jesus' name. Amen.

*Wednesday Morning*

With grateful heart I rise to praise Thee, O Lord, my God, for Thou hast refreshed me with a restful sleep and given me Thy grace to see the dawn of a new day. Thou hast also made this day. It is Thine. Grant that every word I utter and every act I perform will reveal Thy presence in my life. Make me thoughtful and considerate at work, and keep me patient with those who irritate me. Remove from my heart all malice and resentment, and enable me to bear with serenity the unpleasant situations which I cannot change.

Protect me from the allurements of sin, from doubt and worry, from lovelessness and strife.

Throughout this day enrich my life with Thy benedictions. Protect me from accident and harm, and bring me safely home in the evening hour of this day, for the sake of my Lord and Savior. Amen.

*Wednesday Evening*

As the evening shadows fall, closing out the light of the day, come, Thou merciful Savior, with Thy benedictions into my heart, and bring to me the full forgiveness of all my sins and Thy glorious peace which passes all understanding. Relax my body and this coming night give to me the much-needed rest. Remove all worrisome thoughts from my mind, and enable me to sleep undisturbed while Thou art watching over me.

Bless all Thy people far and near, and give healing and strength to the sick. If I have grieved anyone today, forgive me; if I have offended Thee, gracious Savior, blot out these sins; if I have been neglectful and thoughtless, make me different tomorrow.

Protect all Thy children from want and worry, from bitterness and resentment, from strife and anger. Keep us all in steadfast faith, and give me the grace to resist every temptation to sin. Keep me humble and pure in heart. Hear my petitions, almighty Savior and Friend. Amen.

*Thursday Morning*

At the beginning of another day, Father in heaven, it is good to know that Thou hast promised: "As thy days, so shall thy strength be." I cannot tell what this day has in store for me, whether good fortune or misfortune. But I trust Thy promise that Thou wilt give me the strength to bear whatever this day may bring and that Thou wilt make every experience work together for my good.

I am grateful for the opportunities which this day, with Thy blessing, offers to provide my daily bread. Teach me, while toiling for the material things of life, never to forget that my Savior said: "Seek ye first the kingdom of God and His righteousness, and all these things shall be added unto you." May spiritual values be first today in all that I think and say and do. Help me firmly to believe that Thou wilt add to me of things material what Thou knowest to be best for me.

Keep me faithful and true today to Jesus Christ and His religion, and may my conduct glorify Thy name. Amen.


*Thursday Evening*

O eternal God, merciful Father, as the shadows of evening lengthen, I seek the comfort of Thy gracious presence.

I thank Thee for all the blessings which I have enjoyed from Thy bountiful goodness, for Thy protecting care amid many dangers, for Thy favor on my labors, for the love of the members of my family, for everything which has made this day a happy one in my life.

I am especially grateful for Thy love toward me, for the forgiveness of my sins, for the assurance that Thou art my heavenly Father and Jesus Christ is my Savior, for the blessings of my church, and for Thy grace, which has always been sufficient to sustain me.

"Bless the Lord, O my soul; and all that is within me, bless His holy name. Bless the Lord, O my soul, and forget not all His benefits, who forgiveth all thine iniquities, who healeth all thy diseases, who redeemeth thy life from destruction, who crowneth thee with loving-kindness and tender mercies, who satisfieth thy mouth with good things, so that thy youth is renewed like the eagle's. . . . Bless the Lord, all His works, in all places of His dominion; bless the Lord, O my soul." In Jesus' precious name. Amen.

### Friday Morning

Lord God, loving Father, keep me from temptation this day. I know that Satan will not stay away from me and that the example of the evil world will entice me. I do not know what temptations today may bring. Keep me lest I be tempted to take Thy name in vain, to take my work too easy, to lie, or slander, or steal. Preserve me from neglecting opportunities to do good in my work or at home.

Thou, dear Lord, knowest my sinful heart, which so easily departs from Thee. Give me the grace to recognize temptation when it comes, and fill my heart with Thy Holy Spirit that I may resist and overcome sin.

Help me also to regard the trials which may come to me this day as coming from Thy gracious hand, that I may be drawn closer to Thee. Whatever the difficulties in my family or in my work may be, make me strong in hope and trust. Help me to say: "My heart from care is free; No trouble troubles me," knowing that troubles must fade in Thy presence. Help me at all times to look forward to the day when I shall rise above all pain and trouble to the glorious mansions prepared for me by my Lord and Savior Jesus Christ. Amen.


*Friday Evening*

Merciful Savior, as the shadows of the evening lengthen and the darkness deepens, I commit myself and all my loved ones to Thee. Hide Thy face from my sins, and forgive them for the sake of Thy bitter suffering and death. Keep sorrow and harm from me this night, and guard me against fear. Keep also my dear ones who are far away, and guide them in a safe path.

O Lord, have pity on the sin-stricken, and comfort them with Thy Word. Raise the fallen, cheer the faint. In some way bring the comfort of Thy Word to all who will receive it. Let them find a word in Scripture for their present need, or send them a Christian messenger who will point them to Thee. Make all Christians willing to open their hearts, their voices, and their purses, that the Word of Life may be brought to all people.

Give me rest from the labors of the day that I may awake with a strong body and an alert mind tomorrow, prepared for whatever the day may bring. Keep me thankful, hopeful, and cheerful, ever intent on serving Thee and my neighbor. Hear me, gracious Savior. Amen.

*Saturday Morning*

Gracious Father, Caretaker of my soul and Protector of my life, I come to Thee in this morning hour, seeking Thy guidance for the day. I need Thee every moment as I go about my tasks or seek my recreation during the leisure hours given to me. Grant that I may give evidence by word and conduct of my loyalty to Thee and my devoted love to the Savior, who has redeemed me and brought me to faith that I may be a member of His church.

Give me the courage to lift high the banner of the Cross through the sincere profession of my faith and the high standard of my Christian life. Let my chief concern be to give of my time and thought and possessions to the building of my church. Permit nothing to keep me from worshiping Thee in Thy sanctuary tomorrow and confessing Thy Son as my Savior and Lord. In Thy presence let me find forgiveness and peace. Help me to put Thee into the very center of all my interests for the sake of my adorable Redeemer, who died on the cross because He loved me. Amen.

*Saturday Evening*

As this week comes to a close, I praise Thee, Lord Jesus, with my grateful heart for the protection and guidance which I have enjoyed through Thy goodness and love. Thy continuous presence has made the day brighter. Even though I have failed and faltered, Thou hast not turned from me. In Thy loving-kindness blot out each and every sin, and draw me closer to Thy loving heart, where alone forgiveness and peace is to be found. Let not the sins of this day or yesterday cling to me. Then Thine shall be the praise and the glory.

Bless me this night with a refreshing sleep that I may be fully alert tomorrow as I worship Thee at Thy sanctuary. Grant that the Lord's Day message may have a special significance for me and that I, having heard it, may apply it to my life in word and action this coming week. Bless the preaching of the Gospel at all times and in all places, and bring many to hear the saving truth that Thou alone canst set us free from the power of sin, most glorious Savior.

May the peace and the hope of Thy Gospel make us all better Christians, stronger in faith, nobler in character, more consecrated servants and faithful disciples. Abide with me this coming night in Thy grace and mercy, divine Friend and Redeemer. Amen.

## THE FOURTH WEEK

*Sunday Morning*

Heavenly Father, hallowed be Thy name. Help me on this Lord's Day to come into Thy presence with thanksgiving and to join my fellow Christians in hymns of praise and adoration. As I kneel before Thee, my Maker, give me joy in worship and help me to declare before all people that Thou art a mighty and forgiving God. Help me to give the glory which is due Thy holy name. Graciously accept also the offerings of my hands, and use my gifts in the service of my congregation and of Thy church everywhere.

Fill my pastor with a rich measure of Thy grace. Help him to speak Thy Word courageously and convincingly, that the hearts of the hearers may be drawn closer to Thee. Send Thy Holy Spirit into the hearts of men everywhere that they may believe and be saved from sin and damnation. Multiply the number of believers mightily, and give them the courage to confess Thee before men. Give me and my church the grace to believe and to teach Thy Word in its true meaning, and help me and all Christians to pattern our lives according to it.

By Thy Holy Spirit make me pure in heart and mind, help me to worship Thee in the beauty of holiness, and grant that in word and deed I may ever seek to please Thee. Above all else, grant me life eternal through Jesus Christ. Amen.

*Sunday Evening*

Gracious God, I thank Thee for the blessings of Thy Word, through which new strength and comfort have come to me today. Keep me in Thy care, and help me daily to rejoice in the forgiveness of my sins and in the new life and salvation which I have in Thee.

Lord God, heavenly Father, keep and protect me this night, and strengthen me for tomorrow's tasks that I may serve Thee and the people around me cheerfully and well.

Lord Jesus Christ, make me grateful for Thy holy, bitter, and innocent suffering and death, and lead me with Thy gentle Shepherd's hand all my days.

Lord God Holy Spirit, keep me in the saving faith, and strengthen my love and trust that I may walk humbly and serve my God nobly.

O holy blessed Trinity, send Thy holy angels to watch over me and over those near and dear to me. Grant us quiet, peaceful rest and, if it please Thee, a healthy and joyful awakening tomorrow. If in Thy good pleasure this night should be my last on earth, receive me into Thy heavenly glory, where I shall worship and praise Thee forever. Amen.

*Monday Morning*

Heavenly Father, Thy Kingdom come. "Thine, O Lord, is the greatness and the power and the glory and the victory and the majesty; for all that is in the heaven and in the earth is Thine. Thine is the kingdom, O Lord, and Thou art exalted as Head above all. Both riches and honor come from Thee, and Thou reignest over all; and in Thine hand is power and might; and in Thine hand it is to make great and to give strength unto all. Now therefore, our God, we thank Thee and praise Thy glorious name."

Rule this world, Lord, by Thy gracious and almighty power. Restrain the wicked, give the countries of the world honest and peaceful governments, and grant that righteousness and peace may prevail everywhere.

Rule Thy church, Lord, and govern its teachings by Thy holy Word. Bless the teaching of Thy Word that many more people may learn to know and love Thee and that the believers may be strengthened in their faith and in their Christian life.

Rule my heart, Lord, and help me to grow in the knowledge and love of Thee day by day.

Bless my work today, and bless honest labor everywhere. Make an effective witness of me, and use me to bring the good news of salvation to people near and far.

Rule the hearts and lives of everyone that Thy good will may be done in all things; in the name of Jesus. Amen.


*Monday Evening*

Lord, I thank Thee for the blessings which Thou hast graciously given me on this first workday of the week:

   For safety in traveling to and from my place of work;

   For health and strength to be useful;

   For the completion of a task well done and for the approval of my superiors;

   For the pleasant companionship of my associates in work;

   For protection against the physical hazards that accompany my work;

   For the food, clothing, and shelter which my labor has purchased for me;

   For the opportunity to show myself as a Christian to those around me, and for the courage to speak for Thee;

   For these and all other blessings I thank Thee.

Help me constantly to become a better worker. Help me to remember that I am serving not only myself but also Thee and my fellow men. Make me always willing to do a day's work for a day's pay, and to give rather more than less of myself. Give me a peaceable heart in my dealings with others. Help me to love them, and help them to love me, remembering always Thy own great love for me and all mankind.

As I fall asleep, give me joy in my Savior Jesus Christ and the full assurance that in Him I have forgiveness of sins and eternal life. Amen.

*Tuesday Morning*

Lord, gracious and merciful, by Thy Holy Spirit Thou hast implanted into my heart an undying hope which promises rest after the toiling and laboring of this present life and an everlasting peace in the glories of Thy eternity. Look with favor upon me and mercifully help me in the struggles and trials of life. Be Thou with me as I face the hardships and the irritations of the day, the temptations of Satan, and the sins and doubts of my own heart. Graciously take me by the hand and lead me hour after hour in the sunshine of Thy grace. Direct my footsteps on the journey of life to render service to Thee and my fellow men. Keep out of my day all harm and danger of both body and soul. Let me live continually in Thy presence.

I pray for all those who are weary and heavy-laden, for all who are discouraged, for all who mourn and weep, and for all who are lonely and distressed. Draw closer to them and to me with Thy ever-renewing strength, and preserve us all in this saving faith to the end of days, through Jesus, my precious Savior and Friend. Amen.

*Tuesday Evening*

Lord God, my Father in Christ Jesus, I know not what tomorrow has in store for me, but I am not afraid, because I have Thee. Thou hast promised me Thy continuous presence, and that is enough to know. I place myself into Thy care for this coming night, certain that tomorrow Thou wilt be with me as I journey on, performing my daily tasks with gladsome heart and to the glory of Thy precious name.

Save me from the follies and enticements of sin. Keep from my heart all envy, bitterness, resentment, and discontent. Make me to see that each task laid at my door is a privilege, each duty an opportunity, and each assignment a challenge. Grace me with patience, thoughtfulness, and good will toward my fellow workers. May all that I do and say in the tomorrows give honor and praise to Thy Son, Jesus Christ, my Savior and Redeemer. As Thou art with me this coming night, let me be Thine forever. Amen.

*Wednesday Morning*

Thy loving-kindness, O God Eternal, has given me another day of grace with all Thy promises and benedictions. Grant that I may accept it with thankful heart and use each hour to the honor of Thy name. Let not the many vexations of the day rob me of that cheerful and hopeful outlook of life which is mine because of the faith I have in Christ Jesus and in the many promises Thou hast made to me in Thy Word. When discouraged, let me come to Thy throne in prayer and learn again that nothing can separate me from Thy love through Him who was crucified for me, Thy Son Jesus Christ. Abide with me throughout the day, and keep me in Thy grace, and bring me to the evening hour unharmed in body and soul. Forgive me every sin in thought, word, desire, and deed, and let this day be rich in service to Thee and my fellow men.

Then my heart and lips shall praise Thee throughout the day for the sake of Jesus Christ, my Savior and the Lover of my soul. Amen.


*Wednesday Evening*

As the day comes to its close and I once more worship Thee, eternal Lord, my grateful heart comes to Thy throne of grace with songs of adoration and praise. I bow to receive Thy benedictions and acknowledge Thy loving-kindness and guidance as Thou hast blessed the labors of my hands and protected my soul from gross sins. In Thy goodness Thou hast opened Thy hand and hast given me more than I need for today. Thou hast drawn me to Thy heart and forgiven me all my sin and enriched each hour of this day with Thy heavenly peace and the eternal hope which is mine through the sacrifice of Thy Son Jesus Christ, my Priest and King.

Bless me with an undisturbed sleep this coming night, and let no one pluck me out of Thy protecting arms. Hear me as I plead, for the sake of my Savior, the Shepherd of my body and soul. Amen.

*Thursday Morning*

O Lord, my God and Father in Christ Jesus, I thank Thee for the protection of Thy angels through the night, for the rest Thou hast provided, and for the gift of another day to live for Thee.

Keep me humbly dependent on Thee for every good and perfect gift, for Thou art my Father, and I am Thy child.

If it be necessary, send me trials and disappointments so that I may be humbled and kept free from vanity. When Thou dost afflict me, let me not turn away from Thee in despair but remain faithful to Thee in the sure hope that

Thou chastenest those whom Thou lovest and scourgest every son whom Thou receivest.

Keep Thine eyes ever upon me, O Lord, and mine eyes ever upon Thee. Thou hast said: "The steps of a good man are ordered by the Lord." "Order my footsteps by Thy Word, and keep my soul sincere. Let sin have no dominion, Lord, but keep my conscience clear."

Let this day be a day of witnessing for Thee, my Father, and for Thy Son, my Savior, in whose name I come into Thy presence. Amen.


*Thursday Evening*

Heavenly Father, Thy mercies were new this morning, and they did not fail me through the day. Praise and thanks be to Thee for being faithful to Thy promises and unwavering in Thy steadfastness. I am not worthy, Lord, for I have this day been unfaithful and have wavered from the path of righteousness. Forgive me for the sake of the bitter suffering and death of my Savior, Jesus Christ.

Help me to thank Thee as much for my afflictions as for my blessings, for all come of Thee for my good and bring me closer to Thee.

If I have unknowingly wounded anyone this day by word or deed, pardon me. If I have neglected opportunities to bear witness to Thee, forgive me. If I have loved the world too much and Thee too little, take not Thy Holy Spirit from me, but restore unto me the joy of Thy salvation.

As the night closes in on me, surround me with Thy protective strength and almighty care. Remove all fears and dispel all doubts from my heart, lest Satan rob me of some of the certainty of my salvation and the sureness of Thy protection. Keep me steadfast in my faith, and preserve me unto Thy heavenly kingdom. Amen.

*Friday Morning*

Dear heavenly Father, in whom we live and move and have our being, I thank Thee for last night's rest and for the opportunities which this new day brings. May I serve Thee faithfully and diligently. As I perform my tasks, help me to be considerate and kind to those with whom I come into contact. Remind me that all men are Thy creatures and that Thou wouldst have all to be saved. When things go wrong, let me not despair but look to Thee for guidance. Teach me to consider not only earthly values but, above all, eternal values. I wish no greater honor than to be called Thy child. Stay close by me, and watch over those I love. I ask this in the name of Jesus, who shed His blood on Calvary for my sins. Amen.

*Friday Evening*

Gracious Lord God, abide with me, for it is toward evening and the day is far spent. I praise and thank Thee, for Thy goodness and mercy have protected me again today and have brought me safely home to my loved ones. Whatever I have done wrong, forgive, dear Lord. If I have failed in my Christian duty, if I have disobeyed Thy Word, for Christ's sake remove my transgression from me as far as the east is from the west. Let Thy divine care encompass me and Thy faithful disciples everywhere. Bless Thy church in its effort to bring the Gospel to all people. Protect our country with Thy power, and so direct the affairs of men that wars may cease and peace rule the nations of the world. Grant this, dear Lord, for Jesus' sake. Amen.


*Saturday Morning*

Dear Father in heaven, deliver me from evil. Thou hast promised: "There shall no evil befall thee, neither shall any plague come nigh thy dwelling," and yet I know that "we must through much tribulation enter into the kingdom of God." Help me therefore to know that all things work together for good to them that love God.

I know that Thou wilt keep evil from me according to Thy promise. Grant me Thy grace that I may not bring evil on myself by sinning. Spare me from evils of body and soul, of property and honor. When troubles arise, use them to chasten me and to draw me more securely into Thy loving arms. Bless me in my work and in my home according to Thy good pleasure. Make me patient in suffering, helpful to the afflicted, and grateful for all blessings which Thou hast given me. Show me ways of using my talents and powers for Thee and for my fellow men near and far.

Finally, when my last hour comes, lead me safely through the valley of death into the glory of heaven, where Thou Thyself wilt forever wipe away all tears from my eyes.

Thine, O Lord, is the kingdom and the power and the glory forever. Do what is best for me and for Thy kingdom. Make me content. I know Thou wilt do it for the sake of my Savior Jesus Christ. Amen.

*Saturday Evening*

Lord, I thank Thee that Thou hast given me health and strength to conclude another week in Thy service. I thank Thee for all Thy undeserved blessings, for my work, for my family, for Thy daily care and protection, for Thy Word, for peace of mind, for my church, and for my country. Help me daily to remember that all these blessings come from Thee and that without Thee I would be miserable, hopeless, and helpless.

Grant me Thy care and protection also this night. Give me refreshing sleep in preparation for blessed worship of Thee tomorrow in company with fellow believers. Keep me and all others in Thy paths tonight, particularly also the young, and guard them against the sins and follies by which Satan tries to ruin their lives.

Preserve our country in peace. Guard our church against indifference and false teachings, and make our schools nurseries of useful knowledge for the young. Comfort the sorrowful, provide for the poor, and use me according to Thy good pleasure in carrying out Thy work on earth. Show me the needs of my fellow men, and move my heart to works of charity and love.

Each week and each day draw me closer to Thee through saving faith in Jesus Christ, and when this life is ended, receive me into Thy eternal glory. Amen.

ADDITIONAL PRAYERS

## Sunday Morning

Dear heavenly Father, who on the first day of the week didst create light out of darkness, I thank Thee that Thou hast brought me to see the light of another day. Be with me and bless my visit to Thy house today. As I hear Thy Word, clear the darkness of sin from my heart, enlighten my understanding, and quicken my spirit. Create in me a right spirit to praise Thy name and to let my light shine before men.

Blessed Savior, who on the first day of the week didst rise from the grave as my Redeemer from sin, help me with repentant faith to accept Thy forgiveness, daily to rise from sin and to serve Thee in newness of life.

O Holy Spirit, who on the first day of the week didst descend upon Thy church with blessing and power, bless me with spiritual healing, and give me strength to speak the things I have seen and heard.

O holy, blessed Trinity, grant Thy faithful pastors grace to preach Thy Word with power.

Preserve the hearers from distracting thoughts and cares. Enable me with open mind and ready heart to receive Thy truth and to order my life according to Thy Word and will; for Jesus' sake. Amen.

*Sunday Evening*

Accept my thanks, Lord God, for the joy and peace of Thy Gospel message, for the physical rest, the mental refreshment, and the Christian fellowship which I have enjoyed today. Let neither care nor pleasure retard the growth of the seed of Thy Word planted in my heart. Help me to put into practice the sacred truths I have heard. Forgive every thoughtless word or deed with which I may have offended Thee or my neighbor. Never permit the image of Christ to be marred in me through sin or shame.

Keep me and my loved ones also this night from harm and temptation. Grant me restful sleep, and awaken me refreshed in body and spirit tomorrow to meet the challenges of a new day. Give me strength and courage by my speech and conduct to set others a good example as I walk the Christian way of life to Thy glory and for the sake of Jesus Christ, who went about doing good. Amen.

*Morning Prayer*

Heavenly Father, give me this day my daily bread. With all mankind and with all Thy creatures I look to Thee for all my needs. I pray Thee, care for my soul and for my body according to Thy grace and wisdom.

Give me food, drink, clothing, and shelter in the measure in which it is good for me, and make me wholly content. Continue to give me health and work that I may earn my daily bread. Give me a generous heart that out of the abundance which Thou givest, I may help the needy.

O God, I pray Thee also, bless and prosper the members of my family and my friends. Give us a government which rules for the welfare of all. Protect our country, our churches, our homes, our schools, that we may work quietly and enjoy Thy blessings in peace. Help us all to remember that our needs will be supplied as long as we rely on Thee and on Thy bountiful mercy. For all things make me thankful; in the name of Jesus. Amen.


*Evening Prayer*

Gracious Father, as I look back on the day which is drawing to a close, I have every reason to be thankful. I have kept my faith, and by Thy grace I have been able to avoid falling into shame and disgrace. I have come through the day strong in body and mind, and Thy blessing has accompanied my work.

But, dear Father, I have also every reason to be ashamed. My thoughts were not always with Thee as they should have been. Though my outward actions may have pleased people, there has been so much pride and selfishness in my heart that I can only say: "Make me more like Thee." I have missed opportunities to speak of Thy love for lost mankind, partly because I did not watch for opportunities and partly because I was too fearful.

O God, forgive all that has been wrong with me, and draw me closer to Thee. Strengthen my faith and courage, and make tomorrow a better day for me, a day of thanksgiving and service, a day of joy and witnessing, a day of looking heavenward; through Jesus Christ. Amen.


*Morning Prayer*

Eternal Father, in Thy fellowship is health and in Thy grace is forgiveness and peace. By Thy goodness I have life, and through Thy mercies I am sure of my eternal salvation.

Take from my mind all worries and anxious thoughts, and remove from my day the irritations which make for discontent. Break to me enough bread each day, and fill my heart with the earnest desire to obey Thy will and follow in faithfulness Thy Son Jesus Christ, my Savior.

Remove all sin from my imperfect heart, and keep me humble and trusting in Thy grace. Put my mind at ease as I lean upon Thee as the Rock that is higher than I. As I go through the day performing my routine tasks and duties, let me find joy in the things I do, remembering that I am to glorify Thee in all that I say and accomplish. Bless me and those around me. Grant that I may return unharmed to my home to enjoy the benedictions of Thy love. Then my thankful heart will sing the praises of Thy goodness and mercy throughout the evening hours, through Jesus Christ, my Lord and my Redeemer. Amen.

*Evening Prayer*

Lord of heaven and earth, my understanding Father through our adorable Savior, Thou hast so graciously made me Thine own. I praise Thee, for Thy mercies have been greater in number than the countless sands of the many seas. Thou hast removed the burden of my sin, cleansed my conscience from the sense of guilt, comforted me in every frustration of the day, instructed me in Thy Word, warned me against the deceitful enticements of Satan, and ordered my footsteps in Thy ways of peace and joy.

I lift my heart and voice in thanks and praise to Thee and ask Thee to continue to be with me this night. Preserve for me Thy Word, the Gospel, which keeps me in Thy grace. Feed both body and soul in Thy kindness and love. Put my mind at ease, removing all worries and anxieties from my life. Bless me with restful sleep, and when I awake, I still shall be praising Thee, who art my loving Father in Christ Jesus, Thy Son, my crucified Savior. Amen.

*Saturday Morning Prayer*

As I begin this day, I thank Thee, O Father of all mercies, for the blessings of this week now drawing to a close. Thou hast again kept me from harm this night. Also during the past week Thou hast granted me health and happiness. Thou hast forgiven my sin, strengthened my faith, and nurtured my hope of heaven. For these and countless other blessings I am grateful to Thee.

I pray Thee, in Thy mercy accompany me and my loved ones on our path of duty. At work or at leisure, help me to keep myself unspotted from the world, so that with pure heart, kind words, clean hands, and ready feet I may daily grow in Thy service.

Heal the sick, restore the erring, help the troubled, support the afflicted, and comfort the sorrowing. Bless our government, and prosper our nation.

Keep Thy Word constantly before me that it may ever be a lamp unto my feet and a light unto my path. And if I should be called upon to bear a cross, grant that the love of my Redeemer, who gave Himself for me, may give me strength that I may not falter under the load. Stay with me to journey's end. I ask it in Jesus' name. Amen.

*Saturday Evening Prayer*

As the shadows of night settle upon another week about to slip into eternity, I thank Thee, my loving heavenly Father, for Thy merciful guidance and protection in the past, Thy comforting assurances for the future, and the eternal bounties of Thy grace.

According to Thy mercy forgive my failures, and help me more and more to abound in that faith which worketh by love. Grant Thy sustaining presence to me and to all those who are in need of Thy help.

Bless our home, our church, our nation. Give our missionaries zeal and courage to proclaim Thy name boldly before men. Protect our loved ones in the Armed Forces. Grant quiet rest and peaceful slumber this night.

In the morning let me arise refreshed in body and spirit for the services of Thy house, there to sing Thy praises and to be built up in my precious faith. Into Thy hands I commend myself and all men for help, guidance, protection, pardon, peace, and life eternal; through the ever-living Christ. Amen.

*Prayers for Christian Living*

*For More Abundant Living*

Blessed Lord and Savior Jesus Christ, Thou hast warned me that "a man's life consisteth not in the abundance of the things which he possesseth." Teach me to realize ever more that happiness in life does not depend on the measure of material things I may call my own, but on the use I, as a good steward, make of what Thou hast committed to my care.

Grant me the grace to desire not so much an abundance of goods but rather an abundant life of service to Thee and to my fellow men. Show me how to use Thy gifts, both spiritual and material, that my life may bring happiness to me and be acceptable to Thee.

Bless, dear Savior, the work I do for Thy kingdom. Grant me the joy to see the fruits of my labors and of my offerings. Make Thy word, "Give, and it shall be given unto you," true also in my experience that I may be able to continue in the abundant life.

Someday, I pray Thee, let me hear Thee say to me, "Come, ye blessed of My Father, inherit the kingdom prepared for you from the foundation of the world." Amen.

*For Purity of Heart*

O Lord God, who dost delight in a clean heart, I come not relying on my personal righteousness, but trusting solely in the merits of Thy beloved Son, my Redeemer Jesus Christ. For His sake forgive me my sins. Create in me a clean heart, and renew a right spirit within me. Remove from my mind all evil desires. Cast out from my life all greed and envy, all anger and hatred, all pride and vanity. Spare me from an accusing conscience. Fill my soul with love for Thee and a spirit of service to my fellow men. Grant me strength to resist and overcome temptation. Clothe me with the garment of righteousness that Jesus won for me on Calvary. Cause me to grow in grace before Thee and to increase in works of love as long as I live. And when my life comes to a close, give me a place with Thee in heavenly glory. This I ask in Jesus' name. Amen.

*For Readiness to Forgive*

Lord Jesus, I ask with Peter of old: How often must I forgive those who sin against me and offend me? O Lord, if I am to forgive seventy times seven, then Thou must give me the grace and the will to do so. My sinful heart is resentful and often filled with bitterness against others. So often I have been hurt and sinned against. I must confess to Thee, Lord Jesus, that I do not find it easy to forgive and forget. Help me, O Lord.

I know Thou hast forgiven me times without number. That is why I am coming to Thee, asking for help. Enable me in all sincerity of heart to say as Thou didst on the cross: Father, forgive them; and then help me to forgive as Thou hast forgiven me more than seventy times seven.

Hear my plea, gracious Lord. Amen.


*For Finding Peace of Mind
Through Forgiveness*


To Thy Father-heart I come today, Lord God, seeking peace of mind. I am distressed and perturbed, irritated and worried, full of dissatisfaction with myself and the world around me. My sinful heart is rebellious, my day is filled with envy, and my feelings are so easily hurt. I know, O Lord, that I myself am at fault. I have not opened my heart to Thee, nor have I given service and consideration to those with whom I live in this home and to those with whom I must work throughout the day. Everything annoys me, I must confess. Those with whom I work get on my nerves. O God, I admit that it is I, my sins, my lovelessness, which create these situations. Therefore, I come to Thee, asking Thee for grace to conquer myself. Restore to me the desire to walk in Thy presence, and let me live in the sunshine of Thy love.

Forgive me all my sins, and fill my soul with peace. Go with me, Lord, through the day, put my mind at ease, and speak peace to my soul through that reconciliation which is found in the Cross of Jesus, my Savior. Amen.

*For Finding Joy
in My Forgiveness*

Blessed Father in heaven, who art abundant in goodness and truth, forgiving iniquity, transgression, and sin, I thank Thee for the grace and mercy assured me by the redemption of Thy Son. In Thy fatherly love look down on Thy disloyal child. "Cast me not away from Thy presence, and take not Thy Holy Spirit from me. Restore unto me the joy of Thy salvation, and uphold me with Thy free Spirit." Have mercy on me for Christ's sake, and forgive what I have done wrong and what I have left undone. Quiet my troubled conscience with the knowledge of sins forgiven. By faith in Christ fill my heart with the joy of adoption into the family of heaven. Engraft me as a living branch upon Thy Son, the Vine, that I may bring forth fruit in abundance by leading a holy and blameless life to the glory of Thy name and for the benefit of my fellow men. Help me ever to live in Thy favor and finally to die in Thy peace; for the sake of Jesus Christ, my Lord and Redeemer. Amen.

*For Overcoming My Worries*

Lord God, my heavenly Father, who hast made all things by the Word of Thy power, I, Thy unworthy creature, give Thee praise and honor. Though the immensity of Thy creation overwhelms me, Thou hast assured me of Thy infinite and continuing love. In Thy mysterious mercy Thou hast seen fit to give Thine only Son into death for my sins that I, believing in Him, might become Thy adopted child and an heir of eternal life.

As I struggle with my petty problems and am troubled by the worries that beset my pathway through this world of sin, grant me the assurance that Thou art my loving Father and I Thy cherished child by faith in Christ. Free me from the anxieties of life. Lift me up from the depths of despair. Give me grace to accept the forgiveness Thou hast provided for repentant believers. Cause me in the midst of every difficulty and trial, every sorrow and woe, to trust Thy providence and to look to Thee alone for help. And make all things work together for my everlasting salvation; through Jesus Christ, my Lord. Amen.

## *For Overcoming My Fears*

Lord God, heavenly Father, "whom have I in heaven but Thee? and there is none upon earth that I desire beside Thee. My flesh and my heart faileth, but Thou art the Strength of my heart and my Portion forever!"

I am deeply grateful that Thou art my God, who hast promised never to leave me nor forsake me. I trust Thy Word that nothing shall be able to separate me from Thy love which is in Christ Jesus, my Lord.

I am ashamed to confess that sometimes my heart is filled with fear as I look at the trouble and turmoil in the world today. Sometimes I am afraid to face a difficult problem in my personal life. Forgive my little faith. Increase my faith in Thy loving-kindness and in Thine almighty power that I may overcome my fears and meet every trying experience with confidence. Make Thy strength perfect in my weakness.

By Thy Holy Spirit enable me confidently to say, "I will fear no evil, for Thou art with me." In Jesus' name. Amen.

## For Overcoming My Doubts

Lord, I am troubled by many things, and sometimes I fear for my faith. In my sorrows I am inclined to forget Thee, and in bodily weakness I sometimes doubt Thy ability to help. In health and prosperity I am inclined to forget Thee and to ascribe my successes to myself and to my hard and intelligent work. I know that all this shows weakness of faith, sinful pride, and forgetfulness of Thee. I must say tearfully: "Lord, I believe; help Thou mine unbelief."

Gracious Father, help me always to remember that Thou art God; that Thou hast given me my body and soul, my food and clothing, home and family, and all that I have; that Thou defendest me against all danger and guardest and protectest me from all evil; not because I deserve it, but because of Thy fatherly goodness and mercy.

Help me always to remember, Lord Jesus, that Thou art true God and true man; that Thou hast shed Thy holy precious blood for me to redeem me from sin, from eternal death, and from the power of the devil, that I might be Thine forever.

Help me always to remember, Lord God, Holy Spirit, that Thou hast called me by the Gospel and brought me to faith in my Lord and Savior Jesus Christ, that I have forgiveness of sins and eternal salvation through such faith, and that Thou hast promised to keep me in the saving faith until my dying day.

Yes, Lord, help me to remember what Thou hast graciously done for me, and in that remembrance help me to trust in Thee for all my needs, never doubting that Thou art my God and that I am Thy beloved child. In that knowledge help me to live joyfully and confidently, and to die gloriously; through Jesus Christ. Amen.

*For Overcoming My Disappointments*

Lord God, heavenly Father, Thou hast promised that all things work together for good to them that love Thee, to them who are the called according to Thy purpose. Thou hast made me Thy child and an heir of this promise. Strengthen my faith in Thy perpetual mercy and unfailing care. Forgive me for doubting Thy faithfulness and for questioning Thy love. If Thou didst reward me according to my iniquities, surely my lot in life would be nothing but misery and continual heartache. But Thou art gracious and forgiving and dost bless me in spite of my sins.

Help me to understand that my disappointments are not a result of Thy neglect but rather Thy call to repentance and a closer walk with Thee. Continue to correct me when I fail Thee, and keep my eyes upon the crown of glory reserved in heaven for me.

Help me to use my disappointments as occasions for prayer and for humble dependence on Thee, who, together with the Son and the Holy Ghost, art the only true God and eternal life. Amen.

*For Overcoming My Dissatisfaction*

Lord God, life seems to hold and offer so little to me from day to day. Everything provokes me, and my friends seem to be so thoughtless and unconcerned about me. Nothing seems to satisfy me, nothing gives me pleasure. Everything, Lord, is boring and irritating. I know, God, it is I. I need help. My outlook on life must be changed. Thou, Lord God, art the only one able to do this. Therefore, I seek Thee and ask Thee to enter my heart and take full possession of me that I may by Thy grace conquer my depressed moods. Give me full measure of contentment and patience. Create in me a greater willingness to forget self and to be helpful to others.

Let me find in the many promises of Thy Word the key which will open the door to a more satisfying and richer life. Remove from my heart all jealousy and selfishness, and show me how I can be a blessing to others and helpful to the discouraged. Forgive me for complaining, and help me to count my blessings day after day. Make me appreciative of Thy benedictions, and keep me in Thy grace. In Thee and in Thy Son, Jesus Christ, my Savior, let me find my most complete joy and contentment and peace. Help me, O Lord. Amen.

*For Overcoming My Sensitiveness*

Dear Savior Jesus Christ, I am much troubled by a serious personal fault which makes life hard for me and for those around me. I know that Thou hast redeemed me from sin and damnation and that this is reason enough for me to be kind, cheerful, hopeful, and helpful. Yet I am altogether too sensitive in my daily dealings with relatives, friends, and with associates in my work. I am inclined to regard every adverse word or criticism as an insult. As a result, relations are often strained, and life is a burden instead of a glorious adventure.

I do not want to be like that, Lord. I want to be normal like other people. I want to be able to take the irritations of life calmly. I know the fault is mine. I am proud when I ought to be humble, selfish when I ought to be helpful, depressed when I ought to be cheerful. I make life miserable for others when I ought to be kind and helpful.

When I look at Thee, my Savior, who wast reviled but didst not revile, who wast despised but didst not despise others, who wast abused but who didst serve others in life and in death, I am thoroughly ashamed of my childish, selfish behavior. Turn my heart, and make me what I ought to be. Give me a new outlook that I may rejoice in the welfare of others, spend my life in the service of others, and be a blessing wherever I go.

Lord, when I think what Thou didst for Saul the Pharisee, for Zacchaeus the tax collector, and for countless others, I know that Thou canst also make me over into a pleasant and useful person whom others will be glad to have in their company. I trust Thee to do it, merciful Savior. Amen.

*For Overcoming My Self-Pity*

Lord, I know that I am easily hurt and feel myself slighted and passed by as I meet associates at church and at the many social gatherings in the community. It seems as though no one cares for me. Therefore I feel sorry for myself and think that I am mistreated and ignored. Lord, help me to conquer this morbid outlook on life, and create in me a deeper interest in my fellow beings, looking away from myself and seeking to be useful to others. Grant me the grace to be less self-centered and self-conscious. Forgive me my murmurings, and make me cheerful and friendly.

I know I am precious in Thy sight, for Thou hast given Thy Son as a sin offering for me. Thou, O Lord, art thinking of me and of my eternal welfare. Grant that this truth will help me to conquer my self-pity. Let me not continue to bemoan my lot in life. Open my eyes to see that where I am I can serve Thee and be of real service to mankind. Thou hast called me by name. I am Thine own. May I rejoice daily to know that my name is written in the Book of Life. Let me count my blessings as an heir of salvation. Give me the satisfaction of sharing with others the saving truths of the Cross and telling them of Jesus, the Savior, who sacrificed His life that they, too, might be Thine through all eternity. Abide in my heart for the sake of Jesus, my Savior and Friend. Amen.


*For Overcoming My Intolerance*

Lord God, heavenly Father, Thou knowest that I love Thee. I pray Thee in the name of Jesus Christ to make me understand that if I love Thee, I must love my neighbor also.

The world around me is often indifferent toward the poor, and prejudiced against those of another race or color. Banish from my heart all thoughts of pride and prejudice, and implant in me the spirit of tolerance and good will to all.

Help me to be more than merely tolerant; help me to love those who are in need of my love, no matter who they may be. Keep me aware that Thou hast created them all of one blood to dwell on the face of the earth, and that Thou hast sent Thine only-begotten Son into the world that *"whosoever* believeth in Him should not perish, but have everlasting life." Forbid that I should ever by an intolerant word or deed offend anyone Thou hast loved and for whom Thy Son, the Savior, has died. Teach me, by Thy Holy Spirit, to be more like Thee with every passing day also in loving my neighbor of another race or color.

Cause the spirit of humility and tolerance to increase among men that all may live together in this world in peace and good will. In Jesus' name I pray. Amen.

### *For Relief from Frustration*

Gracious God, who dost search the hearts of men and knowest their thoughts altogether, "create in me a clean heart, and renew a right spirit within me. Cast me not away from Thy presence, and take not Thy Holy Spirit from me. Restore unto me the joy of Thy salvation, and uphold me with Thy free Spirit."

Teach me to say with the Psalmist: "Why art thou cast down, O my soul, and why art thou disquieted within me? Hope thou in God; for I shall yet praise Him, who is the Health of my countenance and my God."

"Search me, O God, and know my heart; try me, and know my thoughts; and see if there be any wicked way in me, and lead me in the way everlasting."

If my frustrations arise from a rebellious and dissatisfied heart, forgive me, Lord. If my restlessness arises from my failure to look to Thee for rest, teach me to come to Jesus with my burdens and lay them at His feet. If those who dislike me succeed in making me miserable, help me to rise above this pettiness and to be strong in Thee and in the power of Thy might. If Thou art testing me, give me the strength to bear my burdens, for Thou hast borne the burden of my sins for me. Help me to know the godliness with contentment which comes from Thee alone, for Jesus' sake. Amen.


*For Grace to Adjust Myself*

Gracious God, heavenly Father, I must confess that I am at times upset by the many changes that come in life. I find it difficult to make the necessary adjustments. I do not ask to understand, but help me, I pray Thee, always to realize that no matter what happens to me, and what changes must be made, Thou dost still love me and wilt make every experience work together for my good.

Give me the faith to trust Thy promise, "My grace is sufficient for thee." In mercy forgive all grumbling and complaining of which I have been guilty in the past. Teach me to follow the example of Jesus, my Savior and Lord, who also in trial and tribulation said, "Not My will, but Thine, be done." In that spirit I shall be able to meet whatever life has in store for me. For Jesus' sake. Amen.

*For the Grace of Humility*

Most righteous and everliving God, whose standard is perfection and whose justice punishes sin with consuming fire, I bow before Thy majesty and humble myself in Thy holy presence. Make me understand that the way of the transgressor leads to eternal disaster. Impress Thy will upon my heart. Grant me true repentance. For Jesus' sake forgive my sins and shortcomings, my ignorance and hardness of heart. Give me grace to pattern my conduct after Thy Word. Destroy in me the spirit of pride. Make me realize the gravity of my sin so that I may humbly cast myself upon Thy mercy. Preserve me from the spirit of the Pharisee who would exalt himself above others. Incline my heart to be merciful to all men. Enable me out of sincere gratitude for sins forgiven to crucify my flesh and to excel in Thy service. And by Thy mercy grant that I may finally enjoy the light and joy of heaven; for the sake of Jesus Christ, Thy Son, our Lord. Amen.

*For Grace to Be Patient*

Divine Savior, how patient Thou hast been with me! Times without number I have failed Thee, yet Thou hast not turned from me, but with a compassionate look Thou hast sought me and drawn me to Thy forgiving heart. How thankful I am that Thou hast tenderly pleaded with me through Thy Word and Thy Christian church! Grant that I may learn from Thee to be patient with others, thoughtful and considerate, even though they irritate, upset, and disturb my peace of mind. Remove from my heart all resentment toward those who provoke me by word and action, not returning evil for evil, unkindness for unkindness, harsh words with caustic rebuttals.

When Thou, gracious Savior, wast mistreated, misunderstood, hurt and bruised in body and sorrowful in soul, Thou didst pray: "Father, forgive them." Grant me the grace to face the many vexing problems of the day with patience and find in Thee rest and peace and contentment. Let me lean on Thee for strength and guidance and abide Thy time, Savior and Lord. Amen.

*For the Grace
of a Consecrated Life*

O Lord, my God, Thou hast said: "I have redeemed thee. I have called thee by thy name. Thou art Mine." Praise and thanks be to Thee for having loved me with an everlasting love and for having drawn me to Thee with loving-kindness. Thou hast spared not Thine own Son, but hast delivered Him up to the cruel death of the cross that I might be Thine own and live under Thee in Thy kingdom. What shall I render unto Thee for all Thy benefits toward me?

Lord, give me a thankful heart and a daily determination to live like Jesus, who died for me and rose again. Help me to live my thanksgiving by a reverent and cheerful obedience to Thy will and by a steadfast trust in Thy loving-kindness and unfailing mercy.

Help me to be what Thou dost want me to be, and when I fail, forgive me for Jesus' sake. Let Thy daily pardon strengthen my daily perseverance to love Thee and my fellow man.

Thou, O Lord, hast called me out of darkness into Thy marvelous light. Give me the grace to live as a child of light and an heir of heaven, that men may glorify Thee and be drawn to Him who is the Light of the world, Thy Son, my Lord. Amen.

*For the Grace
to Be True to Myself*

Dear Father in heaven, I thank Thee for all endowments of body and mind. Help me to make the most of them, and help me to be myself, which I often find hard or impossible. Too often I want to be someone else, to imitate others, forgetting that Thou desirest me to use my talents as Thou hast given them.

Teach me to recognize that my failure to make the most of myself is often due to jealousy or to a mistaken sense of values. I want to do as my neighbors do, though my earthly means do not permit me to live according to their standards. The outward glamour of certain people or occupations sometimes causes unrest in my heart. Sometimes I aspire to be what I cannot or should not be. I sometimes lose my sense of gratitude for what Thou hast made me and given me, and as a result I become unpleasant or unhappy.

Help me first of all to understand myself, Lord. Help me to see who I am and what I can do, and then give me the courage and endurance to develop my talents and powers and to be wholly myself. Help me to see Thy beauty and wisdom in the diversity of talents and powers, and help me and others to use the diversity of gifts which Thy gracious hand has bestowed for the joy and benefit of all people.

Yes, Lord, help me to find myself and to develop myself that I may serve the purpose for which Thou hast created me. Above all, strengthen my faith and trust in Thee that I may remain Thy child in all eternity; through Jesus Christ. Amen.

*For the Grace to Make
the Right Decisions*

Heavenly Father, who knowest all things and seest the end from the beginning, Thou art never at a loss as to what to do next. The marvels of Thy creation and the miracles of Thy providential direction of the affairs of men and nations testify to the infinite wisdom with which Thou dost order all things.

I humbly confess that I am often perplexed by the problems of life. Sometimes I do not seem to know which way to turn next. I pray Thee, therefore, to enlighten me by Thy Holy Spirit that I may recognize what is Thy will in every situation; give me the courage to decide every issue accordingly and to leave the final outcome to Thy direction.

Especially do I thank Thee, heavenly Father, that Thy Spirit has brought me to make the right decision concerning Thee, my God and Savior. I have been richly blessed in the faith that Thou art my heavenly Father and that Jesus

Christ is my Savior. Do Thou keep me steadfast in this faith to the end, and then give me, according to Thy promise, the crown of life. For Jesus' sake. Amen.

*Gratitude for the Blessings Received*

Heavenly Father, Thy goodness has opened Thy hands to supply me with the needs of this day, and Thy love has protected me from harm and danger and injury. But Thou hast done more; Thou hast opened Thine heart and drawn me closer to Thyself with Thy forgiving mercies. Truly, Thou art wonderful, O God, merciful Father! Make me appreciative every day of Thy many blessings. Let me count them one by one with a grateful heart. May I at no time forget Thy benefits when a desire of my heart has not as yet been granted. Too often I have forgotten to thank Thee for everyday blessings. I arose this morning and could walk; I opened my eyes and could see; I reached for my food and could enjoy it. O Lord, many are Thy blessings. Who could count them all?

But how often I have forgotten to thank Thee for peace of mind, for cleansing from sin, for the air we breathe, the refreshing water we drink, the beauty of Thy creation which we can behold! Lord, make me truly grateful and appreciative as I count my blessings each and every day.

Above all, I thank Thee that Thou hast given me a Savior who walks with me, cleanses me from sin, and guides me daily in the paths of righteousness. In Thy grace let me live today with thankful heart, for Jesus' sake. Amen.

*Gratitude for Special Blessings Received*

Almighty and eternal God, of whom and through whom and to whom are all things, I join my voice with the chorus of the angels and the glorified saints assembled around Thy throne in ascribing to Thee blessing and honor and glory and power.

I am unworthy of the least of Thy blessings. And yet in Thy mercy Thou hast given me life. By the precious blood of Thy Son Thou hast called me into Thy kingdom at my Baptism. Thou hast redeemed me. Thou hast sanctified me by Thy Spirit and renewed me in Thy image. Thou dost daily and richly forgive all my sins. Innumerable, O Lord, are Thy spiritual blessings.

I am richly blessed also materially. Thou hast given me health, surrounded me with the beauties of Thy creation, supplied me with friends and loved ones, and endowed me with wonderful personal gifts and abilities. Thou hast singled me out for special blessings not shared by others. I have not always recognized or appreciated them as I ought. Teach me to recall them and to number them one by one. Help me daily to place them at Thy feet and to dedicate myself anew to Thy service; for Jesus' sake. Amen.

## *Gratitude for the Joy of Being a Christian*

O God, I thank Thee for the saving faith in Jesus Christ, my Savior, and for the privilege of being a Christian. Give me a deep and abiding faith, and grant me the grace to show in all my actions and in all dealings with my fellow men that Thou art the Ruler of my heart and mind and that the joy of salvation is the dominating influence of my life. Keep me from becoming discouraged by the troubles and cares of this life, and make me trusting, cheerful, and confident. At the same time keep me humble always in the knowledge that salvation is from Thee and that heaven is Thy gift.

In gratitude for the salvation which Thou givest, help me to live and die in the spirit of the psalmist: "I will extol Thee, my God, O King; and I will bless Thy name forever and ever. . . . Great is the Lord and greatly to be praised; and His greatness is unsearchable. One generation shall praise Thy works to another and shall declare Thy mighty acts. I will speak of the glorious honor of Thy majesty and of Thy wondrous works. . . . The Lord is gracious and full of compassion, slow to anger, and of great mercy. The Lord is good to all, and His tender mercies are over all His works. . . . My mouth shall speak the praise of the Lord; and let all flesh bless His holy name forever and ever." Amen.

*For Conquering Alcoholism*

Lord Jesus Christ, Thou art the Strength of my soul, and in Thee do I hope. Without Thee I can do nothing, but all things are possible to those who trust in Thee.

Give me the grace to see my sins of intemperance as rebellion against Thy holy will, as a crucifixion anew of Thee, and as a grieving of Thy Spirit, whose temple I am. Cut away from me all satanic webs of self-defense and pitiable excuses, and help me cry: "O wretched man that I am, who shall deliver me from the body of this death?"

Give me the faith wholly to lean on Thee. Strengthen my trust in Thy grace, which is sufficient for my weakness. Bestow Thy strength upon me when my will power fails. Guard me in the hour of temptation, and give me the power to resist the urge of intemperate appetite for strong drink. In Thy name I ask it. Amen.

*Prayers for Christian Worship*

*For the Joy of Worship*

Heavenly Father, let me share the joy of the psalmist who said, "I was glad when they said unto me, Let us go into the house of the Lord." May every opportunity offered to worship Thee in Thy house find me eager to join in hearing Thy Word, in singing Thy praise, in lifting up my heart to Thee in prayer.

May Thy Holy Spirit so bless the hour of worship in Thy house that I may be refreshed after the toils and burdens, the sins and failures of the weekday world. I need so much my Savior's invitation, "Come unto Me, all ye that labor and are heavy-laden, and I will give you rest."

Teach me to come into Thy presence with a contrite heart, and let me depart with the knowledge that my sins are forgiven. Fill my spirit with the peace which the world cannot give.

*From Thy house when I return,*
*May my heart within me burn,*
*And at evening let me say,*
*"I have walked with God today."*
*Amen.*

## Before Going to Church

Gracious Savior, who hast made each Sunday a day of triumph through Thy resurrection, increase in me the desire to worship Thee as my adorable Lord and merciful Savior. Grant that the message of Thy redeeming love, which I shall hear today, may make me more appreciative of Thy grace, strengthen my faith, ennoble my character. Make me more faithful in this coming week that I may be able to resist all temptations which come my way. Make me ever more willing to serve my fellow men as Thou hast served me. Remove all distracting thoughts from my mind, and let me apply all that is said to myself rather than to others.

Let my attendance at Thy house of worship be an example to others that they, too, may come and share with me the peace and hope which are mine through Thy Gospel of love and grace. Pour out upon me Thy richest blessings now and always, most gracious Savior and Friend. Amen.

## After Attending Church

With thanks and praise in my heart, O Lord, I return from the service where I have worshiped Thee today, confessed Thy name and my faith, and made my prayers. Thou hast spoken to me through Thy Word, assuring me of the forgiveness of all my sins. These promises sent me on my way rejoicing as my heart is filled with peace and the certainty of salvation. Thou hast shown me the way that I should go, warned me against the pitfalls of sin, and given me directives for my Christian living. Grant that I may daily reduce to practice the things which I have heard. Let Thy Word bring forth in me fruit an hundredfold to the glory of Thy name.

Bless the ministry of my pastor. Watch over all the members of my church, and lead them daily into the paths of righteousness. Help me to dedicate myself to Thee in a richer and fuller service and share with my fellow Christians the responsibility placed upon us by Thy Son Jesus Christ.

Open more doors of service to me, and let me enter gladly and serve Thee with all the ability Thou hast given me by Thy goodness and love.

Bless me daily with Thy benediction, and let Thy presence guide and protect me throughout this week. In Jesus' name I ask this. Amen.

*For Baptismal Grace*

Lord God, heavenly Father, Thou hast redeemed me, Thou hast called me by my name and hast said: "Thou art Mine."

Praise be to Thee for having received me as Thy child in Holy Baptism. Thanks be to Thee for having washed away all my sins, for making me a partaker of all the blessings of Thy grace, and for bringing me to faith in Thy Son through this washing of regeneration and renewing of the Holy Ghost.

By Thy Holy Spirit keep me in my baptismal grace. Arouse me daily to heartfelt contrition and repentance so that I may never spurn Thy grace through indifference and unbelief. Stir me up daily by this grace to a life of holy obedience to Thy will.

In my moments of temptation and doubt cause me to rest my hope upon the grace bestowed on me in Holy Baptism. Thou wilt ever remain faithful to Thy responsibilities as a heavenly Father. Keep me faithful to my responsibilities as Thy child. And when I fail, do not cast me aside, but for the sake of Thy Son and my Savior pardon me and help me to improve. Keep me in Thy grace until I meet Thee face to face. Amen.


*For My Communion Sunday*

As I desire to approach Thy table, precious Savior, make me worthy and acceptable, mindful that Thy grace alone gives me the privilege to partake of this blessed Sacrament. I have sinned, I have been discouraged, I have given way to needless worries, I have questioned Thy promises,

I have been of a doubtful mind. I confess all these and other shortcomings and ask Thee to receive me nevertheless and to blot out all my transgressions against Thee and my fellow men. Create in me a clean and pure heart, a greater faith, and the grace to walk with Thee in that way which leads to life eternal. Draw me to Thyself with Thy constraining love, and send me on my way rejoicing because of the forgiveness and peace which I have received at Thy table of love and grace. Preserve me in this union with Thee and the fellowship of those with whom I have shared this blessed meal. Continue to be with me and all Thy people until journey's end, most gracious Savior and Lord. Amen.

*For Bible Sunday*

"Thy Word is truth," gracious Lord and Father, the only truth which makes us wise to salvation through faith in the crucified Savior. I praise Thee, Lord God, for this revelation of Thy love and the saving Gospel of my redemption through Jesus' blood. May nothing be more precious to me than Thy Word. May I at all times reach for my Bible when I need guidance and counsel, comfort and strength, healing and forgiveness. Help me to grow in understanding and knowledge of Thy revelation and feel at home with Psalms and Prophets, Gospels and Epistles.

Grant that the number of those increases who daily read Thy Word and find through Christ of Calvary peace of heart and mind and directives for Christian living. May I at all times speak of this hope which is in my heart and continue to grow in knowledge of Thee and Thy will; for Jesus' sake. Amen.

*For a Better Understanding of My Bible*

Gracious Lord, I thank Thee for Thy Word of salvation, for it is a lamp unto my feet and a light unto my path. Grant that I may love it, understand it, believe it, and live according to it.

Make the Bible my comfort and guide. Open my heart and mind when I read Thy Word that its sacred message may take root and grow. Help me to regard all faithful pastors and teachers as Thy representatives, and strengthen my faith through their preaching and teaching.

Teach me to regard Sunday not only as a day of rest from my labors, but also as a day on which I may gladly hear and learn Thy holy Word.

Help me on this day, and at all times, to seek and find Thee as Thou hast revealed Thyself in the Scriptures. Grant that I may daily worship and glorify Thee as my Creator, my Redeemer, and my Comforter; through Jesus Christ. Amen.

## On Joining the Church

Dear heavenly Father, who through Thy Son Jesus Christ hast brought me into sonship with Thee, I thank Thee that Thou hast led me to the knowledge of Christ as my Savior and through Him hast introduced me into the larger fellowship of the Christian church. Now that I have become a member of the church, help me to be faithful to my baptismal vow, diligent in the performance of the duties I have undertaken, and steadfast in my associations with my fellow Christians.

Give me grace, I pray Thee, to be an effective witness of my faith in word and deed. Preserve me from any lapse of my discipleship. Inasmuch as I have received greater knowledge, enable me to render greater service to Thee and to all those with whom I may come into contact. Cause me to be an active, energetic builder in Thy kingdom, not for self but for Thy glory and the salvation of precious souls. Inspire me to let my light shine here until I shall see the light of Thy glory there. Grant this for Jesus' sake. Amen.

## Taking an Office in the Congregation

Lord Jesus, Bishop and Head of the Christian Church here on earth and King of kings on the throne of eternity, my congregation has honored me by choosing me to serve Thee in a special capacity of our congregational life. The ability to perform my duties well and acceptably comes from Thee and depends upon Thy benediction. Give me a ready heart and willing hands and a truly Christian vision to grasp each and every opportunity to serve Thee, confess Thee as my Savior, and serve my fellow men within and without the church.

May I at no time forget that I am rendering this service to Thee, and am not merely to please people. Let me experience daily the satisfying joy of doing things for Thee. If it be Thy will, grant that I may also see the fruits of my labor. Allow nothing to discourage me nor rob me of this zest and zeal which is put into my heart by Thy Holy Spirit. Preserve in our congregation the unity of peace, that with one accord we pursue the tasks which lie before us. Then Thine shall be the praise and the honor and the adoration from my grateful heart, now and always. Amen.

*For New Year's Day*

At the dawn of this new year, precious Savior and divine Lord, I desire to begin this day in Thy name. Therefore I ask Thee to take full possession of my life, hold me by the hand and lead me from day to day, protecting me from all dangers of body and soul. Shield me from the temptations of sin and remove every doubtful thought from my mind. Let not the worries and fears of the future rob me of that peace of mind which is mine through Thy sacrifice on Calvary. Order my footsteps in the paths of uprightness, and keep me in Thy grace.

Abide with Thy children wherever they are, and help them through their trials and troubles. Forgive us, one and all, our many sins of the past through Thy cleansing and precious blood. Grant me and all that love Thee the strength to live victoriously every day.

Give to Thy church, eternal Savior, continued growth, and prosper the work of our hands as we seek to win souls for Thee. Bring this saving Gospel to many more. Preserve peace among the nations that Thy message of reconciliation may not be hindered in its progress as missionaries go from place to place. Let me live in peace with my fellow men, avoiding discord, strife, and hatred. Give me an unwavering faith in Thee as my Savior and King. Make this year another year of grace to me and to many, for Thy name's sake. Amen.

*For the Epiphany of Our Lord*

O gracious God and Lord, who by a star didst lead the Magi to see the manifestation of Thy love for all mankind in the Christ Child, I thank Thee for this revelation that also the

Gentiles should share in the salvation which Thou hast prepared in Jesus Christ, Thine only-begotten Son.

Enable me by Thy Spirit to find peace and joy in the faith that I, too, have been redeemed by Jesus Christ from all sin, from death, and from the power of the devil. Let me never forget that I am now Christ's own and that it is my duty to live under Him in His kingdom and serve Him in righteousness all the days of my life.

Graciously reveal Thyself to all people who even now do not know Jesus Christ and salvation in Him. Gather Thine elect from all the nations of the world that Thy house may be full, and Thine shall be the kingdom and the power and glory forever and ever. Amen.

*For the Lenten Season*

Gracious God, Father of my Lord Jesus Christ and also my dear Father, I thank Thee that Thou hast permitted me to see another Lenten season, during which I am privileged again to meditate on the Cross of Christ with its many comforting spiritual lessons. May this holy season bring me rich personal blessings. Cause the message of the slain Lamb of God to impress upon my heart and mind the awfulness of my transgressions and to lead me to Calvary for pardon and peace. Lead me to see that my sins caused

His great agony in the Garden; that my transgressions nailed Him to the Cross of Calvary; that He was forsaken by His own that I might not be forsaken of Thee; that He died so that I might not die eternally.

O Lord Jesus, grant that especially during this sacred season the story of Thy wondrous love for me may draw me closer to Thee so that in gratitude for Thy great love I may rejoice in my redemption, walk with Thee in willing obedience, and follow Thy example of love and sacrifice.

O Holy Spirit, during this Lenten season grant all pastors a double measure of Thy outpouring to arouse the indifferent listeners, to stir up the lukewarm, to encourage the timid, to assure the doubting, to calm the disturbed, and to console the sorrowing. May troubled souls everywhere by the message of Lent be led to sincere repentance and trusting faith in the Cross of Calvary, so that, dying to sin, they may live to Thee now and forever. In Jesus' name. Amen.

*For Palm Sunday*

Lord Jesus Christ, Lord of lords and King of kings, on Palm Sunday in the long ago the multitudes at Jerusalem hailed Thee with their glad "Hosanna to the Son of David! Blessed is He that cometh in the name of the Lord! Hosanna in the highest!" But a few days later the people shouted their angry "Crucify Him! Crucify Him!" O God, forbid that I should ever be so unfaithful to Thee, my Savior!

Abide in my heart, Lord Jesus, and rule as my Lord and King. Enable me, I pray Thee, by Thy Holy Spirit to remain steadfast in my loyalty to Thee. Keep me also from presumptuous sins, lest I crucify Thee anew with unholy living. Above all the temptations of the unbelieving world, let me hear Thy gracious promise, "Be thou faithful unto death, and I will give thee a crown of life."

Hear my prayer, Lord Jesus! Amen.

## For Good Friday

O Thou Lamb of God, slain for sinners, this day brings me to the foot of Thy Cross. Humbly and shamefully I admit that Thou hast borne my griefs and carried my sorrows; the chastisement of my peace was upon Thee, and with Thy stripes I am healed. I thank Thee that Thou didst suffer all as my Substitute.

For me Thou didst endure the treachery of Judas; the mockery and mistreatment of Herod; the miscarriage of justice before Annas, Caiaphas, and Pilate; the scourge, the rod, and the crown of thorns. For my sins Thy hands and feet were pierced with nails, Thy lips tasted of the vinegar and gall, Thy side was pierced by the spear.

Here I behold the tremendous price of my transgressions that cost Thee Thy life, Lord Jesus. Here I see Thee as the Lamb of God, who by one sacrifice hast forever perfected them that are sanctified. May Thy Cross ever be the source of my forgiveness, comfort, joy, and peace.

As I again view Thee today suspended on the cross of Golgotha, may I by Thy love be prompted to say with Paul: "I am crucified with Christ . . . and the life I now live in the flesh I live by the faith of the Son of God, who loved me and gave Himself for me." Bless the preaching of Thy Cross everywhere, and by its constraining love draw all men to Thee that they may live with and for Thee forevermore. For Thy holy name's sake I ask it. Amen.

*My Easter Prayer*

Lord Jesus, risen and everliving Savior, with Thy people of all ages and races I adore Thee as my Lord and my God, who hast crushed Satan's head, conquered sin and death, and redeemed all mankind from the forces of evil. Accept my hallelujahs as I rejoice with believers, saints, and angels because Thou hast come forth triumphantly from the grave to live forevermore. I ask Thee to cleanse my heart from all sinful desires and dwell therein with Thine eternal peace.

I rejoice to know that Thou hast blotted out all my transgressions and reconciled me with Thy Father in heaven, that I as a child of His household may seek His face and know that He is full of tender mercies and boundless compassion.

I praise Thee because of the hope that Thou hast brought to my heart. I need not be afraid of death and dying because there is no condemnation for us who believe in the saving power of Thy Cross. To all who are sorrowing let this Easter Day bring the comfort of Thy promises and a new joy of expectancy as they look forward to the day when they shall be reunited with their loved ones in the eternal glory of heaven.

I rejoice today because I know that Thy church shall go on from victory to victory, receiving strength from Thine almighty hand. Even the gates of hell shall not prevail against Thy church. Accept my vows of allegiance this day as I dedicate myself anew to Thy service to tell the nations of the earth that Thou art the risen King of the ages.

Take full possession of my heart, remove all sin, scatter all doubts, drive away all worries. Let Thy Spirit set aglow in me a love that will not die. Increase in me day after day the desire to follow Thee to whatever place Thou shalt lead me, until I stand before Thy Throne to behold Thy glory as the risen Lord, and praise Thee with saints and angels with an undying and perfect love. Hallelujah. Amen.

## The Ascension of Our Lord

Lord Jesus Christ, who wast delivered unto death for my offenses, raised again for my justification, and crowned in glory at Thy ascension, I praise Thee for having finished the work given Thee by Thy Father for my redemption and my coronation.

As once Thy disciples gazed steadfastly into heaven as Thou didst ascend on high, lift my eyes heavenward and set my affections on the eternal treasures reserved there for me. O Thou who hast ascended on high and hast led captivity captive, take fuller possession of my soul, my life, my all, so that I may look constantly to Thee as the end and aim of my life.

Strengthen in me the longing for fulfillment of Thy promise: "Where I am, there shall also My servant be." Keep me in the true faith, so that I may ever be prepared for Thy second coming and return to Judgment, ready to meet Thee in the clouds of heaven when Thou dost return in glory to take me to Thy glory.

Let Thy ascension strengthen me in the assurance of my ascension on high, and lift me above the cares and worries of this life. Until Thou dost return, give me the grace and joy of knowing that Thou dost rule all things for the ultimate well-being of Thy dear children. Grant me the cheerful readiness to submit myself to Thy mighty protection and loving direction, and help me daily to crown Thee as my Lord by a life of holy obedience to Thy will. Amen.

*For Pentecost Sunday*

O Holy Spirit, who on the great day of Pentecost didst descend upon the apostles and set their hearts on fire with Thy blessings, I pray Thee to enter my heart daily through Thy Word and stir me up to wholehearted devotion to my Lord and Savior Jesus Christ. Open Thou my lips to testify to the living hope which Thou hast begotten in me through the risen Christ. Give me courage and boldness to speak Thy Word with power so that more people everywhere may know the Father, the Son, and Thee, the Holy Ghost.

Bless the preaching of the Gospel everywhere, and through it conquer the hearts of men for Christ, their King. Graciously attend the work of Christian pastors and teachers throughout the world that by their ministry many souls may be added daily to Thy church. Grant zeal and understanding to Thy church so that the people of God may be warmed to greater service to all mankind.

Enlighten my understanding, control my affections, purify my ambitions, and sanctify my actions, that men may see my good works and glorify my Father in heaven. Keep me repentant over my sin and trustful in my Savior. Comfort me in my afflictions, and preserve me from any sin whereby I might grieve Thee. O Holy Spirit, enter into my heart with Thy blessings and into my life with Thy direction. Amen.

*For Trinity Sunday*

Eternal Lord, who hast revealed Thy majesty, glory, and greatness as Father, Son, and Holy Spirit, I fall before Thy throne with angels and saints of the ages in awe and wonderment. Thou art a great God and *my* God and Lord. I come to Thee, heavenly Father, in the humble faith created in my heart by Thy Holy Spirit. In that saving faith in Jesus, who has redeemed me through His Cross, I am Thine by grace. Accept my adoration and praise, my "Holy, holy, holy," and touch my lips and heart and make them clean. I confess that Thou art the only revealed God and hast spoken to me through Thy Word and Thy Son Jesus Christ.

Preserve me in this saving faith, and give me the grace to confess Thee and Thy Son and the Holy Spirit as my God. Let me never be ashamed of Thee nor deny Thee. Keep my soul from sin, and let me live daily in the sunshine of Thy love.

Then throughout eternity my lips shall praise Thee, Thy grace and Thy majesty, as Creator, Redeemer, and faith-preserving Spirit. Amen.

*For Mother's Day*

Dear heavenly Father, Thou hast said through Thy prophet, "As one whom his mother comforteth, so I will comfort you." I thank Thee for Thine infinite love which so surpasses human understanding that to make it more real to me Thou didst compare it with a mother's love for her child. On the strength of this assurance, I know that I shall have Thy constant guidance, help, support, and protection.

On this day, set aside to honor mothers, I thank Thee especially for the gift of Christian mothers. Bless them always. Give them grace ever to set a good example to their households. Make them constantly mindful that their children are a sacred trust from heaven. Hold Thy protecting hand over them, and give them strength for every task, courage for each trial, and trust in Thee that daily will grow stronger.

I thank Thee particularly for the gift of *my* mother and for her love, which has often comforted me. I ask Thee to help make me worthy of it. May I never do anything that would grieve her heart. May I follow always the path which she has charted — the path which leads to Thee. Guide Thou our footsteps that we walk in the love of Jesus, who set an example by His love for His mother. This is our prayer in His name. Amen.

*For Father's Day*

Gracious God, Father of my Lord Jesus Christ, and through Him also my true Father, I thank Thee that Thou hast given me an earthly father. As Thy representative he has provided me with all that I need to support this body and life, and he has also given careful attention to my immortal soul.

On this day, set aside for honoring fathers, I pray Thee to impress all fathers with their responsibility as heads of their households. Help them in holiness and industry to provide for the physical needs of their families. And grant them grace to rear their children in the way of Thy blessed Word.

I pray Thee, make me increasingly aware of the great debt I owe my father. Help me to cherish him as Thy precious gift. May I always honor him with my love, my respect, and my devotion. Let me not depart from the paths of righteousness in which he has led me from infancy. Cause him as a Christian father to find happiness in my attempts to translate his precepts and example into a life of unselfish service.

Finally, when life's day is done, grant me the joy and bliss of spending eternity with Thee, my heavenly Father, and with him, my earthly father, as well as with all my loved ones.

In Jesus' name I ask it. Amen.

## For Reformation Day

Lord God of hosts, who art the Refuge of every sinner and the Strength of all who put their trust in Thee, I praise Thee for having made me a partaker of the blessings of the Reformation.

Without any merit or worthiness on my part, Thou hast sent Thy Holy Spirit into my heart and brought me to faith in Thy dear Son, Jesus Christ. Thou hast made known to me the worthlessness of my own good deeds and the perfect merit of Christ. Thou hast directed my faith away from the commandments of men and caused me to rest my hope only and solely on the exceedingly great and precious promises of Thy Gospel. Thou hast revealed the beauty of Thy grace, which rescued me from a just condemnation and assured me of certain salvation in Christ.

Grant me Thy grace that I may receive Thy forgiveness with thanksgiving and reflect Thy mercy in thanks-living. Use me as Thy witness in bringing the message of pardon in Christ to my fellow men everywhere.

Open my eyes to a better understanding of Thy Word and a deeper appreciation of Thy grace that my faith in Christ Jesus may grow and flourish with the fruits of righteous living.

Grant purity of doctrine and practice to Thy church that men may be rescued from all human errors and be led into all truth by Thy Spirit. Hear me for the sake of Him who is the Way, the Truth, and the Life, Thy Son, my Lord. Amen.

*For Thanksgiving Day*

With a heart full of appreciation because of Thy goodness and with thanksgiving in my soul for Thy boundless grace, I come on this national Day of Thanksgiving, God of loving-kindness and mercy, to join with heart and voice all the people of this country to praise and adore Thee as a wonderful God and understanding Father in Christ Jesus. Throughout the year Thou hast opened Thy hands and poured out upon me blessing after blessing. Thou hast provided me with all that I need to sustain body and life. Thou hast opened Thy heart and drawn me closer to Thyself, blotted out all my sin, cleansed my conscience from guilt, and spoken peace to my heart. Richly and abundantly Thou hast offered to me Gospel and Sacrament, that my soul be healed, my faith strengthened, my character developed, and my life directed. Accept the thanks and praise of my grateful heart. I sing of Thy goodness, I shout for joy because of Thy mercies.

Let my thanksgiving, however, go beyond words and give evidence in the sharing of my blessing with the hungry, the needy, the lonely.

Give me the grace to continue to praise Thee as a thankful child of Thy love and with all the family of Thy household to serve Thee with faithfulness and loyal devotion through Jesus, my Savior and Friend. Amen.

*For Christmas Eve*

Almighty God, heavenly Father, I thank Thee for Thy unspeakable gift to mankind in the birth of the Christ Child at Bethlehem, as announced by the angel this holy night. May the mystery of the Word made flesh fill my soul with wonderment and yearning that like the shepherds I may make haste to worship at His manger bed. Change my heart from a busy inn that has no room for Thy Son, that it may be a quiet chamber kept for Him.

Help me in the spirit of true repentance to rejoice in my Savior's birth that in genuine faith I may join in the song of the angels, share the delight of the shepherds, and adore Him with the Wise Men. Grant that Christ may be born again to me this holy night that the truth, love, and redemption He brought may henceforth abide in my heart and life. Like Mary, may I keep all these things and ponder them in my heart always.

And as Thou hast made me a partaker of His glory here, grant that I may share His glory there. In Jesus' name I ask it. Amen.

*For Christmas Day*

O God the Father, I praise Thee for the gift of Thy Son, who was born in the poverty and lowliness of Bethlehem so that I might enjoy the riches of Thy grace and the exaltation of sonship with Thee.

O God the Son, I adore Thee for humbling Thyself to be my Savior, for bearing my sins in Thine own body, and for rendering to my Father in heaven a perfect satisfaction for my transgressions.

O God the Holy Spirit, I glorify Thee for having made my heart a dwelling place of the Savior of the world and for bringing the peace of forgiveness to my soul through faith in Him who is the Prince of Peace.

O blessed Trinity, on this holy day give me a humble and contrite heart that I may joyfully claim the Babe of Bethlehem as my Lord and my God. Remove from me the tattered robes of my own righteousness, and adorn me with the spotless garment of Christ's righteousness.

Use every gift received this day from loving friends to remind me of the gift of a Savior so that my heart may rejoice and my tongue can sing, "Glory to God in the highest!"

Help me to cradle the Christ Child in my heart, O Holy Spirit, and give me the grace and strength to love and adore Him all the days of my life. Amen.

## For New Year's Eve

Heavenly Father, daily Caretaker of the souls of men, put Thy protecting arms around me as I enter this new year of grace. Guide me safely through harm and danger which may come my way, protect me from accident and sickness, and preserve me in that saving faith which will make me more than conqueror over all temptations, doubts, and unbelief.

Tonight I am mindful of my many sins and transgressions and ask Thee to blot them out, every one, by Thy love and mercy through the precious blood of my redeeming Savior. In Thy loving-kindness draw me closer to Thyself that I may walk with renewed determination and strength in Thy paths of righteousness, where peace of mind and the hope of heaven are my treasures and my joy.

Preserve in our community Thy saving Gospel and prosper the work of the church established by Thy Son, Jesus Christ, my Savior, that the community and the ends of the earth may know that there is no other name which saves but that of Thy Son, our crucified Savior and Lord.

Thou, O God, hast been good to me through the years, and in Thy mercy Thou hast forgiven me my sins day after day. Grant me the grace to continue steadfast in this saving faith and to walk as it becomes a child of Thy family, through Jesus Christ, my eternal Redeemer. Amen.

*For the Pastor*

Lord Jesus, Thou Chief Shepherd of the sheep, I thank Thee for giving our congregation a pastor who is faithful and true.

Keep me grateful to him

> For preaching Thy Word in truth;
> For his fellowship in the Gospel;
> For his influence in our community;
> For the example of his Christian life.

May I always be aware of my obligation to pray for my pastor, to honor him, and to support him in his ministry among us. Bless him and continue to make him a blessing to me and to the work of Thy kingdom.

Help my pastor and the people of our congregation to be steadfast in the faith, and at last take us all into the Church Triumphant above.

I pray in Thy name. Amen.


*For the Congregation*

I am grateful to Thee, Lord Jesus Christ, that Thou hast established Thy church on earth, where Thou dost bless me with love and mercy in the Word and the Sacraments.

I am grateful that Thy Word is proclaimed in our congregation in truth and purity. May the Holy Spirit fill the members of our congregation that it may be said of us "they continued steadfastly in the apostles' doctrine and fellowship, and in breaking of bread and in prayer." Help me to do my part to keep it so for my own spiritual good.

Use our congregation for the building of Thy kingdom on earth. Make our congregation a power for good in our community, and bless our efforts to bring Thy saving Gospel to the unchurched, to the glory of Thy name.

Hear my prayer, O Jesus. Amen.

*For the Sunday School
and Its Classes*

Lord Jesus, Thou Friend of children, who hast commanded Thy church, "Suffer the little children to come unto Me, and forbid them not, for of such is the kingdom of God," we pray Thee to look with favor upon the efforts of our congregation to bring up our little ones in the nurture and admonition of the Lord. We commit our Sunday school, its teachers and officers, its pupils and visitors, to Thy divine care and guidance.

Grant, we pray Thee, Thy blessing to the instruction offered in our Sunday school. Cause its teachers always to be impressed with the importance of their work, since theirs is the privilege of molding souls for eternity. Give them wisdom and grace to teach the way of salvation in such a clear and compelling fashion that our children, whom Thou hast bought at the price of Thy holy blood, may be ready and eager to receive it. Help them also by personal virtues and exemplary lives to support the instruction they give in the classroom.

Since Thou alone canst give the increase, we ask Thee, dear Lord, to cause the good seed of Thy Word to bring forth fruit an hundredfold in the hearts and lives of our Sunday school children. Give them ready and teachable hearts. Cause them to seek their Creator in the days of their youth. Make them abound in faith, hope, and love. And, having been trained up in the way they should go, may they ever abide in it, and even when they are old never depart from it. Grant this for Jesus' sake. Amen.

*On Opening of School Term*

Gracious Father, I thank Thee for the schools of learning which are opening their doors for another term. Bless the millions of children and young people who are beginning a new school year, and fill them with a love for learning and with a desire to develop their powers to serve Thee. Bless their teachers with true wisdom and with love for Thee, and keep them from teaching anything which might hinder or prevent the proper moral and spiritual development of the students under their care. Make all schools nurseries of useful knowledge, and fill all educators and students with a deep sense of devotion toward Thee.

Hold Thy protecting hand especially over the Christian schools of our country and the world. Give the teachers in these schools a deep insight into Thy saving Word, and make them effective witnesses for Thee, convincing teachers of Thy Word, and wise counselors to the immature. May their testimony and teaching bring peace and comfort to countless hearts. May their example strengthen the students in their determination to place themselves into Thy service. Increase the number of Christian schools and teachers, and make them an ever greater power in the building of Thy kingdom.

Help students and teachers to see all knowledge in relation to Thee. Grant that they may use their knowledge in developing the resources of the earth according to Thy will and for the benefit of man. Give us all the true wisdom which finds its joy in Thee and in the salvation which we have through Jesus Christ. Amen.

## *By the Teachers of the Church*

Lord, Thy blessings are so rich and many that I find myself overwhelmed in thinking about them. I thank Thee that Thou hast permitted me to become a teacher in the church. Help me to perform my work quietly and unselfishly. Help me to prepare my lessons with only the one thought of serving Thee and of leading souls closer to their Savior. Help me to appreciate Thy blessing and guidance more and more.

Bless the work of all teachers in the Sunday schools and in other classes of Christian education. When they become discouraged, lift their tired spirits; when they experience difficulties in their work, lead them to happy solutions; when they see little result of their work, remove the curtain from their eyes and show them the rich fruits of their labors; and at all times keep them humble and cheerful in their work of love.

Lord, in all things guide the instruction of our youth, and give all who have a part in it a right spirit of consecration and love. Grant that their instruction may be heeded, to the salvation of many souls; through Jesus Christ. Amen.

## *By the Youth of the Church*

Dear Father in heaven, who lovest young and old and who carest for them all, I thank Thee for Thy steadfast love and the mercies which come to us day by day. Together with all believers I adore Thee and praise Thee as the Lord of all and the Savior of lost mankind.

At this time I pray Thee especially for myself and all the youth of the church. Thou knowest the many temptations that come to young people. Though Satan may smile at us, he does so only to beguile us. Though the world seeks to charm us, it does so only to mislead us. And even our own hearts are sinful and unclean, as are the hearts of all mankind. I pray Thee, therefore, show me and all young people a special measure of Thy grace, and lead us in right paths.

Help us grow in the love and use of Thy Word. Help us find godly friends and companions who will support and uphold our Christian faith. Give us an understanding of what is right. Move our hearts to want to do what is right, and crown our desire to serve Thee with fruits of godly action. Guard us against the temptations of youth, against irreverence, pride, lust, disobedience, and dishonesty. Turn our hearts to Thee and our thoughts heavenward. Give us a faith that surmounts ridicule and a courage that overcomes any obstacle which may be placed in the way of our faith. Strengthen us in Christ, and keep us with Christ until the day when we shall see Thee face to face in the full radiance of Thy glory. Amen.

*By Youth Workers*

Lord Jesus, Savior of old and young alike, I thank Thee for the youth of the church with their faith and enthusiasm, and for the mature people who guide the young. I pray Thee, give faith to both young and old, obedience to Thy Word, and an earnest desire to serve Thee.

Look with favor on me and on all youth workers, especially on the youth workers in Thy church. Help us to understand young people ever better, to guide them toward the achievement of their hopes and aspirations, to teach Thy Word in ways which are meaningful to them, to set for them a good example, to counsel them wisely, and in every way to lead them on the paths which Thou hast walked.

Give us due patience when young people seem unresponsive to our training efforts. Help us to remember the impulses and desires of our own youth, that we might the better understand the people with whom we work. Make us charitable, helpful, kind in all things. Give us a self-sacrificing spirit, even when our labors may at times seem thankless, that the youth of the church may be preserved in the faith, that converts to Thy name may be won, and that the future of the church may be secure. Hear me, gracious Savior. Amen.

## By Camp Workers

Lord God, Creator of all life and beauty on earth, I thank Thee for all the gifts of Thy love. Help me more fully to appreciate the bounty which Thou hast given, and help me to impress others with Thy marvelous goodness.

As a camp worker I am to help others see the beauties of nature. I am to lead them in various forms of recreation and in other camp activities. Make me competent and adequate for the work at hand. Give me a creative mind, and help me to develop ideas and programs through which Thy name will be glorified and through which the campers will be led to greater appreciation of Thee and to greater love for Thee.

Help all with whom I work and play to enjoy nature and to find spiritual and bodily relaxation at camp. Relieve our tensions, refresh our minds, and strengthen our bodies. Above all, renew and strengthen our faith in Thee, keep us from sin in our work and play, and send us back to our homes strong and confident in Thee.

Guide and lead me in all things that I may do nothing to hinder the spiritual and physical growth of those for whose welfare I am responsible, and grant that I may leave nothing undone which will serve their welfare. Hear me in the name of Jesus, my Savior. Amen.

*For the Missions in Foreign Fields*

Gracious God, Father in heaven, Thou wouldst have all men to be saved and come to the knowledge of the truth in Christ Jesus, the Savior. But "how shall they believe in Him of whom they have not heard? And how shall they hear without a preacher? And how shall they preach, except they be sent?"

Make me zealous therefore, dear Lord, to do my part to send preachers of the Gospel into all the world. Since I cannot go personally, make me glad to support with my money the foreign missionary program of my church. Add my prayers and my gifts, heavenly Father, to those of other Christians, and bless their use in keeping laborers in the fields which are white unto harvest. Accompany the preaching of our missionaries with Thy divine benediction that the borders of Christ's kingdom may be enlarged and the earth be filled with the knowledge of Thy glory as the waters cover the sea.

Hear my prayer for the sake of Him who died that all might live, even Jesus Christ, my Lord and my Redeemer. Amen.


*For Missions at Home*

O Thou who didst come to seek and to save the lost, give me a heart that yearns like Thine for the souls of lost mankind. Thou hast earned a perfect salvation for every sinner by Thy holy life and bitter death. Thou hast made known the riches of Thy grace in the Gospel. Thou dost count on me to make Thy Gospel known to all nations and hast promised to be with me in every mission endeavor.

Preserve me from all selfishness, stinginess, and indifference, lest men perish in their sins for want of the Gospel which I have failed to bring them. Give me a love for souls, a liberal and joyful spirit of giving, and a readiness to support the work of missions with fervent eagerness.

Bless the preaching of the Gospel in this my native land. Give the power of Thy Holy Spirit to the testimony of our Christian pastors, teachers, and all Thy people everywhere. Stir up the hearts of the people of our country so that they will be restless without Thee and may turn to Thee to find peace and rest for their souls.

Lord Jesus, Thou hast given me the command to bring Thy Gospel to every creature. Thou hast promised to be with me. Give me the grace to be obedient and the readiness to follow Thee in the search for souls whom Thou hast redeemed with Thy blood. Amen.

*For Missionary Zeal*

Blessed Lord God, who by Thy Son didst command me to go into all the world and to preach the Gospel to every creature, increase my faith and zeal that I may more earnestly desire and more diligently seek the salvation of my fellow men. I confess that often my heart is cold and my ears are dull to Thy mission cry. I have by no means deserved to be called into Thy church and to be privileged to become Thy messenger. Forgive my indifference for Jesus' sake, and by Thy Holy Spirit fill my heart with a burning zeal to bring the light of the everlasting Gospel to benighted heathen both at home and abroad.

Grant me also a loving heart, sincerity of speech, and piety of life to adorn my Christian profession of faith. May I never by ungodly conduct or unbecoming speech give unbelievers an excuse for criticizing the Gospel of Christ.

Knowing that the day is far spent and that the hands on the clock of time are advancing toward midnight, may I by Thy Spirit's prompting support the mission program of my church with my personal witness, my earnest prayers, and my sacrificial gifts. And grant that through me many may be saved from the kingdom of darkness for the kingdom of Thy Light, through Jesus Christ, Thy Son and our Lord. Amen.

*For the Spread of the Gospel
by Radio and Television*

Lord Jesus Christ, blessed Savior, how great is Thy mercy that Thou wouldst have all men to be saved and come to the knowledge of the truth! Keep me mindful of Thy command to "go into all the world and preach the Gospel to every creature" that men everywhere may learn to know the truth of Thy saving love.

I must confess that I have not always been as active as I might have been in obeying Thy command. At times I was even tempted to excuse my inactivity by pleading that there was little that I could do to bring the Gospel to every creature. But now Thou hast given us the marvels of radio and television, by which the story of Thy saving love can be quickly carried into all the world. Accept, O Christ, my gratitude and my offerings for these modern ways of going quickly into all the world with Thy saving Gospel.

Favor with Thy divine benediction the radio and television mission of our church, and by the working of the Holy Spirit make Thy Word, carried by the air waves, a power to salvation in the hearts and lives of people everywhere, for whom Thou didst die that they might live forever. Amen.

*For Ability to Witness*

Lord, I thank Thee for the saving faith and for Thy promise of eternal life. Make me ever grateful for these blessings and increase my willingness to serve Thee, especially to witness of Thy gracious love for fallen mankind.

I pray Thee, support me with Thy power as I witness to my fellow men. Too often I have missed opportunities to speak for Thee. Forgive me where I have failed. Help me to see opportunities for witnessing, and give me the courage to speak up.

Increase my concern for lost souls and my desire to witness, and strengthen me according to need. Lord, I often do not know what to say, but Thou knowest; I am often weak and afraid, but Thou art strong. Make Thy love my love; Thy words my words; and Thy strength my strength. Help me to speak the right word at the right time, and with all Thy children on earth help me to go forth to new victories for Thee; in Jesus' name. Amen.

*For the Unconverted*

Jesus, Lover of souls, Shepherd of all who stray and err, Thou dost not desire that any should perish but that all should come to Thee and find healing from sin, peace of mind, and cleansing from the guilt of conscience. I come beseeching Thee for my friends who still live without hope in this world and who have closed their hearts and lives to Thy gracious invitation to come and find rest and peace for their souls.

Grant me the grace to avail myself of every opportunity by word and conduct to bear witness to Thee and Thy love. May all my decisions and interests show my associates that I put Thee first in my life and thought. May my behavior at all times reveal Thy gracious presence in me. Make me thoughtful, considerate, helpful, and patient in their presence. Open the eyes of my companions to see the wonders of Thy love, the blessedness of belonging to Thee, and the joy and satisfaction that service rendered to Thee gives to me each day. Abide with me, and bless each effort of mine to win souls for Thee, most adorable Savior and Friend. Amen.

*For a Specific Person
to Whom One Desires to Witness*

Lord God, who givest all things, I thank Thee for all spiritual and earthly blessings which have come to me from Thy gracious hand. Make me appreciative and useful, and grant that I may always be intent on serving Thee. Supply my daily needs, and grant that I may receive the gifts of Thy goodness with thanksgiving. Help me in all things to put Thee first, to seek Thy glory, and to love and serve my neighbor as myself.

At this time I pray Thee especially to give me a courageous and a wise heart that I may witness of Thy love to _____, who is little interested in the needs of the spirit and his (her) own salvation. Give me the right thoughts to think and the right words to speak, and send Thy Holy Spirit into his (her) heart that he (she) may listen and believe. I feel altogether inadequate for the task which is mine to perform, but I know that through Thee I will be able to do all things. Help me to take courage from the example of the apostles, who trusted in Thy promise: "It shall be given you in that same hour what ye shall speak; for it is not ye that speak, but the Spirit of your Father which speaketh in you."

I depend on Thee. Lend power and conviction to my halting words, that ------------------------------- may find eternal life and joy of salvation in Thee; through Jesus Christ. Amen.

*For the Spiritual Welfare of Friends, Relatives, and Fellow Workers*

Dear heavenly Father, who hast so ordered this world that I do not spend my days in lonely solitude but hast surrounded me with family, friends, neighbors, acquaintances, and fellow workers, I ask Thee to look with favor on all whose lives touch mine in the course of my daily activities. Grant them a deep and lasting sense of their sinfulness, and for Jesus' sake lead them to genuine repentance. Give them grace continually to seek the forgiveness of their sins and to know the blessedness of those to whom the Lord does not charge iniquity. Shield them from temptation by the Evil One. Fill their hearts with the faith that worketh by love, the hope that maketh not ashamed, the charity that never faileth, trust in Thee that shall not be shaken, patience that endures, and courage that shall always confess Christ. May they surrender themselves to Thy service and, walking before Thee in righteousness and holiness all the days of their lives, constantly dwell in Thy favor and finally die in Thy peace. For Jesus' sake. Amen.

*For Opportunities
for Kingdom Service*

Dear Father in heaven, I thank Thee that Thou hast made me a child of Thine and hast privileged me to help build Thy kingdom. Every day I pray, "Thy kingdom come." With all my heart I want Thy kingdom to come, and I want to do my part that it may come. Show me how I may help to proclaim Thy name and how I may speak of Thy glorious majesty and of Thy wonderful works.

Open a way of service for me in my congregation. I surrender altogether to Thy will. Give me work in which I can serve Thee best. If it please Thee, move those who are entrusted with the administration of the congregation to ask me to serve, or give me courage to go to my pastor and to offer my services. Let me not sit back and wait while I ought to seek opportunities for service.

Lord, give me the courage to witness for Thee at home, in my work, on my vacations, or wherever I may be, that people with whom I live and work may know how much I love Thee. Increase my faith and my love for Thee, and use my witness for the conversion of unbelievers and for the strengthening of believers. Hear me in the name of Jesus. Amen.

*Prayers for the Family Life*

*My Birthday*

Another year of my life has come to a close, and a new day begins for me, Lord God, eternal Caretaker of my life and Lover of my soul in Christ Jesus. Thou hast been good to me through the years. Thou hast given me health and strength, friends and relatives, enjoyments and pleasures, and, above all, Thy Gospel with its many promises of peace and forgiveness. My grateful heart praises Thee.

Give me the grace to dedicate myself to Thee again on this anniversary of my birth, and grant me greater willingness to serve Thee faithfully and continually. Through Thy Holy Spirit make me a loyal member of the church, a worthy citizen of the nation, a dutiful member of the household, and a conscientious performer of my task at work. Let joy fill my heart as I walk in Thy ways, performing my duties and meeting my responsibilities with faithfulness from day to day.

As I receive this new year of grace from Thy bountiful hands, may I use each day to glorify

Thee, serve my fellow men, and find contentment and peace of mind under whatever conditions I must live. Grant that with Christ in my heart, I may live a fuller and richer life, and finally be received unto Thy glory, where I shall praise Thy mercies and Thy goodness forever and ever. Amen.

*Upon My Graduation*

Dear Lord Jesus, who hast been my Teacher and Friend and hast shown me that the fear of the Lord is the beginning of wisdom, I thank Thee for the blessings of the past which have made my graduation possible. Especially do I praise Thee for the support and prayers of my parents, the patience and devotion of my teachers, and the fellowship and the comradeship of my classmates. Thou hast given me the mental gifts and physical health to achieve the goal I have reached and hast blessed my efforts with success.

Forgive me for the opportunities I have neglected, for my failure to do my best in every situation, and for any wrong I have committed during my school life.

Help me to use my talents and improved abilities to Thy glory and for the betterment of mankind. Continue to teach me Thy ways, and give me a deeper understanding of Thy good and gracious will. Bless my growth in grace, and enlarge my opportunities for service. Hear me, Lord Jesus, according to Thy promise. Amen.

*For a Life Companion*

Dear heavenly Father, who hast said, "It is not good that the man should be alone," I come to Thee asking for help to find my life partner. I pray Thee for guidance, for I am Thy child, and Thou art my loving and heavenly Father. As I seek to assume my normal place in life and fulfill my mission among men, I long to share my love with another, to establish a home, and to rear a family. In Thy tender mercy direct me to a congenial, Christian companion who will appreciate me and requite my love. I do not want to be alone, but much prefer to share my joys and sorrows with a beloved mate — one of my faith and my way of life.

Hear my prayer for the sake of Him who blessed marriage by His presence during His ministry on earth. Amen.

*For One Disappointed in Love*

Lord Jesus Christ, Thou art the Lover of my soul and wilt never leave me nor forsake me. Thy tender mercy is from everlasting to everlasting, and Thy truth endureth to all generations.

Thou hast known the frailty and fickleness of men. Thou knowest how often I myself have betrayed Thy love and trifled with Thy goodness. Forgive me, Lord Jesus, for being lukewarm to Thy love, cool to the offers of Thy grace, and forgetful of Thy sacrifice upon the cross.

Help me to be kind, tenderhearted, and forgiving, even as God, my Father, for Thy sake has forgiven me. Remove all bitterness from my heart, and enable me to show true love to the one who has hurt me.

In the midst of my disappointment, give me the grace to be honest with myself and with Thee, lest I become proud and refuse to recognize my own shortcomings. If I have driven human love away by being loveless or unlovable, teach me to return to Thee for pardon and for the warmth of Thy enduring love.

When it pleaseth Thee, give me the love of one who will pattern his (her) love after Thine, and then give me the grace to do the same. Amen.


*On the Day of Betrothal*

Dear heavenly Bridegroom, my Lord and Savior Jesus Christ, on this day of my betrothal I thank Thee that Thou hast helped me find a person to love and serve until death shall part us. I pray Thee, grant that our joy and happiness may remain throughout our lives, and help us always to live not only for self but for Thee.

O Lord, strengthen us and help our love to mature as time goes on that our betrothal and marriage may be a joy to Thee and to all who know us. When Satan would lead us into quarrels and hatred, help us to know that in so doing Satan is opposing not only us but also Thee. Make Thy strength our strength, and help us to overcome the temptations of the Evil One.

Guide my betrothed and me in Thy paths. Keep us chaste and pure in thought and action. Make us of one mind in planning our marriage that such planning may help to draw us ever closer in love. Help our parents to be understanding, and help us to understand them, that together we may look forward to the day of marriage, that nothing in our planning may disturb our happiness.

Make our marriage happy in Thee, and if it shall please Thee to give us children, grant that we may receive them as gifts from Thee and that we may bring them up to love and serve Thee.

O God, I am so happy that I would like to shout for joy. At all times make my joy a pure and holy joy, and let my greatest joy be that Thou art mine and I am Thine. Hear me, Lord Jesus. Amen.

## On Expecting a Baby

Lord, "I will praise Thee, for I am fearfully and wonderfully made. Marvelous are Thy works, and that my soul knoweth right well." I cannot marvel enough when I think of Thy creation and when I think that Thou art also using me to participate in the creation of a child. I humbly thank Thee for the privilege, and I pray Thee, make of me the kind of mother Thou desirest for every child.

Keep me in strength and health during the days of my pregnancy. Help me to live moderately and circumspectly, avoiding sin and everything that might be harmful to the unborn child. Keep me cheerful in outlook, and help both my husband and me to regard the present period of preparation as a joyous one. O God, help us even now to prepare for the responsibilities of parenthood, and grant that we may never do anything to harm our child bodily or spiritually.

In due time make our present joy complete through the birth of a healthy child, and grant us the grace that we may receive the child as a precious gift from Thee. Help us always to regard and treat him as Thy blessing.

When the child is born, give us wisdom to train him right, and keep us from selfishly spoiling him. May we and our child ever be a joy to Thee and the holy angels, and may we together praise Thee in all eternity; through Jesus Christ. Amen.

*On the Coming of the Baby*
*(Mother's Prayer)*

Lord Jesus Christ, Thou Good Shepherd who dost delight in little babes and dost gently lead those that are with young, I thank Thee for Thy marvelous mercy. Thou hast granted me and my husband the gift of a healthy child, and I cannot praise Thee enough for Thy lovingkindness. Thou hast guided the physician, given me strength during my pregnancy and delivery, and sustained me to this moment.

Give me a grateful heart all the days of my life, and enable me to be the kind of mother who will please Thee. Keep me conscious at all times of the holy trust placed in me by the gift of this child, and help me to bring my child up in Thy fear and favor.

Send Thy guardian angels to watch over my little one, and shield him (her) from all danger of body or soul. Bless those who will help me care for my child. Take my child into Thy kingdom, and give him (her) an inheritance with all Thy saints.

O Thou who hast given life to my child, be Thou our Good Shepherd, and lead us in paths pleasing to Thee. Amen.

*For My Wedding Anniversary*

Heavenly Father, on the anniversary of our wedding I come to the throne of grace with a prayer of thanksgiving. I am grateful to Thee for my marriage partner. I bless Thee that by Thy direction the pathways of our lives met and our hearts were united in true love.

I thank Thee, dear Lord, that our love for each other has been preserved and strengthened through the years. In Thy providential way good days and evil, health and sickness, and all other experiences have bound our hearts and lives ever closer to each other and to Thee, our God and Lord.

I confess that I have not always been as kind and thoughtful as I might have been. I regret that I have sometimes been selfish and indifferent. Help me to make amends. Teach me also to be quick to forgive and to forget any fault of my life partner, even as Thou dost remember my transgressions no more for Jesus' sake.

If it be Thy will, grant us additional years of wedded happiness; cause the bonds of love that unite us to become stronger with the passing of time. When our life is done here below, take my loved one and me into the heavenly home above which Thou hast prepared for those who love Thee.

I pray in Jesus' name. Amen.

*For God-fearing Children*

Dear Lord Jesus, who wast once a little child, I thank Thee for the gift of my children. Make me ever aware of my responsibility as a Christian parent. Thou hast entrusted to me the bodily and, especially, the spiritual welfare of my children. Bless my efforts to bring them up in the nurture and admonition of the Lord.

In Thy mercy be near them at all times to guide, protect, support, and comfort them. As in the days of Thy ministry Thou didst call the little ones to Thee, even so let my children hear Thy kind and beckoning voice through Thy Gospel. Make them strong to do Thy will. Help them to continue steadfast in faith in Thee and in love toward one another. Increase their prayer life. Let their conduct be a shining example that will lead others to know and to love Thee. Bless them and make them a blessing to all their associates.

Finally, at the end of their lives make them members of Thy family in heaven. In Thy name I ask it. Amen.

*Thanks for Godly Children*

Dear God, I thank Thee for Thy countless blessings, especially those of my home and family. Thou hast blessed me marvelously with a Christian spouse and with children who are a joy to me. Accept my humble thanks for the comfort and happiness my spouse and children have brought.

I thank Thee that Thou hast so graciously blessed the Christian training of my children. Thou hast made them reverent toward Thee, respectful toward their parents and superiors, and diligent in their work. O God, keep my children in Thy fear and favor. When they sin, lead them to repentance, and forgive their trespasses. When they rejoice, let them rejoice in Thee and Thy goodness. In sadness, cheer them with Thy mercy. In loneliness, comfort them with Thy presence.

Make me and my spouse appreciative and sympathetic parents. Help us always to regard our children as Thy children. Give us Thy grace that we may continue to train them in Thy precepts. Give us the wisdom, love, and forbearance, which are necessary to make us good parents. May our trust in Thee be reflected in the trust of our children. Above all else, bring us and our children into Thine everlasting glory; for the sake of Jesus Christ, our Lord and Savior. Amen.

## *For a High School Son or Daughter*

Dear Father in heaven, I commend myself and all members of my family to Thee. Thou hast graciously upheld us to this day, and I trust Thy promise that Thou wilt continue to uphold and to bless. We need Thy presence every hour.

At times I become unduly concerned about my son (daughter) _____ in high school. I know that Thou hast promised to bless the Christian instruction which he (she) has received, and yet I am afraid that he (she) may give in to the temptations of the world. I plead with Thee, Lord, to go with him (her) at all times. Give the warning from Thy Word when needed. Give him (her) the strength to withstand temptation. Keep him (her) always in Thy comforting care. Help me to overcome my worries by trusting in Thee.

Permit my son (daughter) to participate in the enjoyments of youth in keeping with Thy Commandments. Give him (her) an alert mind to profit from his (her) studies, and prepare him (her) for a life of usefulness. Give him (her) Christian friends who trust in Thee and who support good character. If it please Thee, help him (her) find a Christian spouse who will with him (her) walk the narrow way of life.

Lord, my son (daughter) is Thine. I commit him (her) to Thy gracious guidance and keeping.

Bring him (her) and me and all who are near and dear to me to eternal life; for the sake of Jesus Christ, my Lord. Amen.

*For a College Student Away from Home*

Lord, I thank Thee that Thou hast permitted our son (daughter) _____ to grow to adulthood and that Thou hast blessed the Christian instruction and training of his (her) childhood. I pray Thee, grant that Thy Word may continue to be his (her) daily guide and delight.

I pray Thee also, grant him (her) a realization of the responsibility that goes with a higher education. Help him (her) to view all knowledge in the light of Thy Word. Give success to his (her) training for a life of usefulness and service. Prosper all useful arts and knowledge, and if it please Thee, help my son (daughter) have a part in the advancement of knowledge.

Help my son (daughter) always to have true friends and to enjoy a balanced social life. Give him (her) friends that strengthen Christian convictions, and keep him (her) faithful to Thee and Thy Word. Grant that he (she) may find a Christian partner for life if it please Thee. May Thy love in Christ Jesus kindle his (her) love for Thee and for mankind. Help him (her) to remember parents and friends at home, and grant us a joyous reunion in Thine own good time.

Hear me in the name of Jesus. Amen.

## *Of Parents for a Mentally Retarded Child*

Lord Jesus Christ, how wondrously Thou didst answer the prayer of the woman of Canaan who pleaded with Thee to heal her afflicted daughter! We come to Thee, precious Savior, with a prayer for our child, who is mentally retarded. We are anxious to have _____ develop as a normal child. We know that nothing is impossible for Thine almighty power. Thou canst heal our child if Thou wilt. But we leave everything to Thy holy will.

We confess, however, that our faith at times becomes weak under the stress and strain of this experience. We do not ask to understand, but pray that Thou wouldst by Thy Spirit strengthen our faith in the promise of Thy Word that all things, even our bitterest disappointments, must work together for good to us because Thou dost love us and we love Thee.

We pray Thee, grant to _____ at least enough understanding that he (she) may learn to know and to love Thee as the Good Shepherd who gave His life also for him (her) and who will always care for every lamb of His flock.

Hear our prayer for Thy name's sake. Amen.

*Of Parents for a Physically Handicapped Child*

Lord Jesus, who hast said, "Suffer the little children to come unto Me, and forbid them not," we brought our child to Thee in Holy Baptism. By this washing of regeneration Thou hast cleansed _____ from every taint of sin and made him (her) Thy very own. We are grateful for this blessing.

But we have another care which we would bring to Thee. Thou knowest, O Lord, that our dear child is physically handicapped. He (she) cannot run and play as other children do. We are troubled, too, about his (her) future. We wonder at times, who will care for our _____ when we are gone.

Forgive us such thoughts of anxious cares, dear Lord! Help us and our child to live day by day, and to cast our cares on Thee, knowing that Thou dost care for us all.

In the meantime give us patience and understanding in caring for _____. Make this testing of our faith and trust in Thee be for our and our child's good. We pray in Thy name. Amen.

*Of Parents for Son or Daughter
Who Has Strayed*

Lord God, our heavenly Father, because Thou didst yearn for Thy children when they went astray, Thou didst send Thine only Son to seek and to save the lost. Thou hast a Father's heart and knowest the anguish we bear over the straying of our loved one.

Lord, he (she) whom Thou lovest is sick in his (her) soul. Recall him (her) from his (her) straying, and restore him (her) once more to the joys of fellowship with Thee and to the security which comes to those who rest securely in Thy fold.

Where we have erred, forgive us, Lord. If we have been neglectful, unkind, thoughtless, cold, or unreasonable, pardon us and help us to make amends. Preserve us from an unforgiving spirit and a haughty heart in our relationship with our child. Comfort us by Thy Spirit, and teach us to rely on Thee.

For Thou, O Lord, dost love our son (daughter) much more than we ever could. Thou hast redeemed him (her), Thou hast called him (her) by name in Holy Baptism. He (she) is Thine.

Deal with him (her) according to the multitude of Thy tender mercies, and do not reward him (her) according to his (her) iniquities. Be gracious to us, good Lord, and reunite us before Thy throne of mercy, for Jesus' sake. Amen.

## *In Marital Difficulties*

Lord Jesus, who didst bless the marriage at Cana in the long ago with Thy presence, my wife (husband) and I need the sanctifying influence of Thy presence in our home. We have not been happy. I confess that we have not always lived our wedded life according to Thy Word. We have had differences, ugly scenes, and harsh words. I am ashamed of my conduct, for I, too, have been personally guilty, and I pray Thee to forgive me my transgressions.

Dear Savior, I pray Thee, come into our home and abide there; then we shall be able to overcome our difficulties. Keep me and my wife (husband) aware of the perfect example of Thine unselfish love and service, and make us eager to follow the same also in our wedded life. Help us both to be willing to forgive and to forget, even as Thou in Thy mercy dost forgive us our trespasses and dost remember them no more. Direct me and my life partner to live according to Thy Word that every experience may serve to draw us closer to each other and both closer to Thee. Hear my prayer, blessed Jesus! Amen.

*For One Absent from the Family*

Dear Father in heaven, I come before Thy throne of grace in behalf of _____, who is absent from the family circle. I know Thou art present everywhere; I know that Thou also art present where he (she) is now living. But I would pray Thee today, to let _____ feel Thy sustaining presence while in strange surroundings. Protect him (her) when harm and danger threaten body and soul; be close to him (her) in every temptation. Let Thy Word be a lamp to his (her) feet and light to his (her) path. Increase his (her) faith and trust in Thee and in Jesus Christ, our blessed Savior, in whom we have forgiveness of sins.

Though we are far from one another in the body, keep us close to one another in spirit and united by a common faith in Thee.

At the appointed time grant us a happy reunion with _____ in our family circle, and may every member of our family have a place in the company of the saints in glory everlasting.

Hear my prayer for Jesus' sake. Amen.


*For the Families of Those in Service*

Lord God of the nations and Ruler of all things visible and invisible, I bring to Thy throne of wisdom, grace, and justice the souls of those families who have been separated by the nation's call to service. Help them to adjust themselves to this situation, knowing that Thou art with each one of them as they are separated one from another.

Preserve them in the faith that saves, and let them learn to lean on Thee continually. Let none doubt Thy protecting care, and grant that they will entrust themselves each day to Thee and Thine almighty hands until they be united again to serve Thee with one heart and one soul to the end of days through Jesus, our adorable Savior. Amen.

*For My Family While I Am in Service*

Gracious and good Lord, many perplexing thoughts run through my mind to disturb and irritate me. I know Thou art acquainted with all my thinking. I and mine are precious to Thee. I know therefore that Thou wilt watch over each member of my family and keep us, one and all, in Thy grace. This Thou hast promised to do. Grant that I will not grow cold and indifferent toward Thee because I am not hedged in and protected by the family ties at home. Give me the grace to continue to worship Thee and come to Thy throne of grace in prayer as do my loved ones at home. There we meet, Lord God, even though we be miles apart, to pray to Thee for forgiveness and protection.

Keep our ideals high, our faith strong, and our lives unsullied by sin. Give me and each one of the family the grace to accept with cheerfulness and courage whatever befalls us. Let Thy Word be to us a light and directive at all times. Above all, let the day be not too far off when we can be united in our home and together worship and praise Thee as our heavenly Father in Christ Jesus, who has promised to be with us always, no matter where we are. Hear my requests for Jesus' sake. Amen.

*For One of the Family in Service*

Lord, Thou art a God of peace and desirest that we should live and let live. Thou lovest all mankind — not only a chosen few. I know Thou hast sent Thy Son, my Savior, into the world of sin to bring peace on earth. Yet the wickedness and selfishness of man has brought on wars and strife, death and destruction. I beseech Thee, heavenly Lord, to touch the hearts of the rulers and leaders of the nations with compassion that each may strive to maintain peace among the children of men.

But, O Lord, I beseech Thee especially today to protect _____, who is in the service of our nation. Grant that the faith which is in him (her) from childhood days may remain unshaken through the many temptations that beset him (her). Help him (her) to conquer discouragement, homesickness, and doubt. Stand at his (her) side when tempted to forsake Thee and to sin. Grant that with Joseph he (she) will say: "How, then, can I do this great wickedness and sin against God!"

As I pray for him (her), remind him (her) to pray for me. As we are parted by many miles, let our prayers meet at Thy throne of grace. Return him (her) unsullied in character, unshaken in faith, and ever loyal to Thee, the eternal Caretaker of our lives, and faithful to Thy Son, Jesus Christ, our Savior and Guide. Amen.

*Family Reunion*

Dear heavenly Father, we are gathered here as a family, some from near, some from far. We thank Thee for this privilege of getting together with our own for a few hours of fellowship, recalling past events, and honoring loved ones. As we do so, we are reminded of the blessings Thou hast showered upon us collectively and individually. Indeed, Thou hast been good to us, to one and all, to great and small. Who can enumerate all Thy benefits?

We praise Thee for Thy temporal blessings which are new to us each morning. We thank Thee for relatives and friends, health and strength, prosperity and peace. We also give Thee grateful thanks for Thy guidance, Thy support, and Thy protection by day and by night. But, above all, we express our gratitude to Thee for Thy spiritual blessings — for having brought us to the knowledge of Thy dear Son, who died for us that we might be His own, to live under Him in His kingdom, and to serve Him in everlasting righteousness, innocence, and blessedness.

May Thy Holy Spirit keep us steadfast in faith, that hereafter we may gather as a family in Thy heavenly homeland, where there is no parting and where there are pleasures forevermore.

In Jesus' name we ask it. Amen.


*For Travel by Land, Sea, or Air*

O Lord, my Guide and Guard, who art present everywhere with Thy mighty power, shield me from all danger as I begin my travel. I rejoice with the psalmist: "Whither shall I go from Thy Spirit, or whither shall I flee from Thy presence? If I ascend up into heaven, Thou art there. . . . If I take the wings of the morning and dwell in the uttermost parts of the sea, even there shall Thy hand lead me, and Thy right hand shall hold me."

Give Thy holy angels charge over me to keep me in all my ways. Cause them to bear me up in their hands, lest I be placed into serious peril.

Give me the common sense to be careful and the Christian judgment to abide by those laws designed for my well-being. Preserve me from recklessness, lest I tempt Thee and forfeit the comfort of Thy promises to watch over me.

Go with me on my travels. Be my Companion, and lead me safely to my destination. If death awaits me on this journey, keep me in true faith in Thee that I may reach my destination in heaven, which Thou hast won for me by Thine atonement for my sins. Amen.

*For Families Having Misunderstandings*

1

O Lord, our God, Thou hast said: "Except the Lord build the house, they labor in vain that build it." We have forgotten these words, O Lord, and our home is not a joy to Thee, nor is it a satisfaction to us. We are laboring in vain, because we are not building our home life according to Thy specifications.

Forgive our wrangling and quarreling, our selfishness and pettiness, our suspicions and hatefulness, our lovelessness and unforgiving spirit. Purify our souls by Thy Holy Spirit, and enter into our hearts and home with Thy pardoning grace.

Help us to be kind one to another, tenderhearted, forgiving one another, even as Thou for Christ's sake hast forgiven us. Turn our hearts and minds to Thy sacred Scriptures so that in them we may find the strength through Thy Spirit to show piety at home. Establish us more firmly in our devotion to Thee so that we may worship Thee at our family altar in spirit and in truth.

Bind our hearts together by Christian love, and help us to love one another for the pleasure, happiness, and peace it will restore to us. Amen.

## 2

Lord, I recognize a happy Christian family life as a gift of Thy mercy, and I thank Thee for every blessing which Thou hast given to me and my loved ones. Now Satan has succeeded in creating jealousies and misunderstandings. We want to do what is right, and we want Thy guidance and correction. Do not forsake us in our sorrow, but visit us early with Thy mercy, and restore our happiness. Forgive where we have sinned, and guide us back into a family life and love which is pleasing to Thee.

Help each of us in examining himself to see the causes of the difficulty. Eliminate pride and selfishness from every heart, and help each of us to say, "Forgive us our trespasses, as we forgive those who trespass against us." Help each of us to see the error of his way and to repent first of all before Thee. Make each of us also humble enough to say: "I have sinned, and I am sorry.

Forgive me for the wrong which I have done." Help us all to rejoice again that we are Thy children, who trust in Thee for every blessing of home and family.

Help us to be good examples to one another and to the families round about. Assure us of Thy forgiveness. In gratitude to Thee help us to find peace in anticipation of the glorious harmony which will prevail between us in heaven. In the name of Jesus, our Savior. Amen.

## 3

Gracious Savior, Thou hast come into life and home to bless those who live under our roof in one household. Enrich our lives with Thy presence, and bless us with Thy benedictions of grace. I need Thee, Savior Divine, for we are not a congenial and compatible family. Our misunderstandings are many; daily irritations vex the routine of our household. We get on one another's nerves. Merciful Savior, we need help and guidance and directives. Graciously enter into our hearts, and make us, especially me, more selfless and less self-centered. Above all, teach me to realize that each day Thou art forgiving toward those who have hurt and wounded me. Help me to conquer my petty spirit, my grudges, and my pet peeves. Show me how to appreciate those who are my own flesh and blood, and recognize that they, too, have rights and privileges and deserve consideration. Unite our hearts in Christian love, for Jesus' sake. Amen.

## 4

Heavenly Father, I am ashamed to confess that we have had a misunderstanding in our family. We have quarreled, ugly words have been spoken, and we are angry with one another. I confess that I, too, have been at fault. I have not heeded as I should the admonition of Thy holy Word: "As much as lieth in you, live peaceably with all men." In sinning against a member of my family, I have sinned against Thee.

Forgive me my faults, and help me by Thy Spirit to banish from my mind all thoughts of revenge. Make me ready to forgive and forget, even as Thou in Thy mercy dost remember my sins no more for Jesus' sake.

Make all who have had a part in this quarrel in our family eager for a reconciliation. Help us to adjust our differences in a manner pleasing to Thee. May peace and good will and love be restored to the honor of Thy holy name. For Jesus' sake. Amen.

## 5

Dear Father in heaven, I come before Thee asking for Thy help and blessing. In our family, where there should be peace and harmony and love, there is strife and discord and hatred. I realize that this grieves Thee, and, as a faithful disciple, I desire to do all that I can to bring happiness into our family circle again.

I recognize that I, too, have sinned. I have not always been as kind and patient and understanding toward the members of my family as I should have been. I am truly sorry for my part in bringing about the sad state in our home, and I ask Thee humbly to forgive these great sins through the merit of Thy beloved Son, Jesus Christ.

Help us to be kind one to another, to deal gently with one another's weaknesses, to love Thee more, and to try to do Thy will. Bless our home with Thy abiding presence, and restore the peace and happiness we once knew. Fill the hearts of the members of our family with Thy love so that we may be more charitable in our relations with one another.

Send Him into our home who so frequently graced the home of Mary and Martha in Bethany. In His name we ask it. Amen.

*For the Lonely*

O Lord, my God, Thou hast said: "I will never leave thee nor forsake thee." Yet I feel forsaken and alone. Thou hast assured me that nothing can separate me from Thy love in Christ

Jesus, my Lord. And yet my heart is distressed by a deadening sense of loneliness.

Lord, to whom shall I go? I believe and am sure that Thou hast the words of eternal life. Strengthen me in my faith, and grant me a fuller measure of comfort from Thy presence.

Lord, give me the grace in my loneliness to search my soul as to its cause. If I am lonely because I have refused to give myself in service to others, forgive me for contributing to my loneliness by my own selfishness. If I am lonely because of loyalty to Thee and Thy Gospel, help me to rejoice in my cross-bearing.

Preserve me from all temptations to forget Thy watchful presence when I am alone, lest I fall into sin and shame. Direct my thoughts heavenward, bring me into the fellowship of other believers, and use me as a means of bringing joy and blessing to others.

Teach me to pray: "Why art thou cast down, O my soul, and why art thou disquieted within me? Hope thou in God; for I shall yet praise Him who is the Health of my countenance and my God." Amen.


*For Parents*

Dear Father in heaven, I thank Thee for having made me a parent. I pray Thee, help me fully to realize my parental responsibility and the privilege of rearing children for Thee.

O Lord, Thou knowest that also Christian parents may become fearful when they think of their responsibility to provide for the body and soul of a child and to keep him on the way of salvation. Forgive me when I become fearful, supply all my needs, and help me to perform my work in child training cheerfully and effectively. Give my children intelligent and responsive minds, and grant that I may always teach them what is right and good. Make them receptive to Thy Word; grant them the grace to receive it with joy and to believe in Thy saving love.

Give me a calm and even temperament, and help me to lead my children patiently and surely toward physical and emotional maturity. Make them useful and helpful in all things that, young or old, they may be a joy to Thee and a blessing to Christian people everywhere. Give my husband (wife) and me the grace that we may agree in matters of child training so that together we may lead our children toward heaven and Thee.

Give our congregation a rich measure of Thy grace and the willingness to maintain well-functioning agencies of Christian education as an aid to us in our child-training efforts. May both we and the congregation perform our respective duties joyfully, diligently, and thoroughly, to the glory of Thy holy name and to the salvation of souls. In the name of Jesus. Amen.

*For Children*

Lord Jesus, Thou wast never too busy to pay attention to children, for Thou dost dearly love them. I am happy that Thou dost love me and that Thou hast time to listen to my prayers and to answer them.

I thank Thee that Thou hast made me Thine own. As I get bigger and stronger every day, help me to grow stronger in my faith, too.

Bless my parents, whom Thou hast given me, and help me to honor and obey them, to love and treasure them. Forgive me when I disobey them or when I fail to honor them as Thy precious gifts. Give them wisdom to train me in the good and the right way, and forgive them when they fail.

Bless my home and every member of my family with a strong faith in Thee and true love to one another. Teach me to be kind, unselfish, helpful, cheerful, forgiving, and faithful in my duties.

Help me to be like Thee, Lord Jesus, to grow in wisdom and stature and in favor with God and man. Send Thy angels to watch over me, to keep me from all harm of body and soul. Bless me, and make me a blessing to my family and friends. Amen.

*Prayers for Various Occupations*

*Before Going to Work*

I thank Thee, dear Lord, who dost bless all honest labor, that Thou hast allowed me to see the light of another day and dost equip me for the tasks it brings. Accompany me as I leave for my work. Help me to face the responsibilities of this day with rejoicing.

Remind me that in all things I work for Thee. Whether I eat or drink, order or obey, plan or execute, let all be done to Thy glory. In discharging the duties of my position give me faithfulness to do well the tasks Thou dost set before me. That I may be better fitted for the demands of this day, ever hold before my eyes the great work of my blessed Savior by which He redeemed me for Thee, canceled all faults and shortcomings, and assured me of my place eternally at Thy side. May His infinite sacrifice of love prompt me to sacrifice for others.

Give me grace to see in my profession an opportunity for loving service to others. And in my associations with them make me quick to forgive, sympathetic to their needs, and joyful in their blessings. Grant this for Jesus' sake. Amen.

## On Returning from Work

It is by Thy grace alone, dear heavenly Father, that I have completed another day of work for Thee. I thank Thee for the health and skills Thou hast granted and for the success Thou hast given to my labor.

If I have failed to do my best today, forgive me for the sake of the bitter suffering and death of Thy dear Son and my Savior, Jesus Christ. If I have not reflected my Christian faith in my conduct, pardon me, and help me to be a better witness to Thee tomorrow.

Thanks be to Thee, Father in heaven, for the protection of this day and for a safe return to my home, which Thou hast preserved while I was at my work.

Grant me renewed strength and vigor for another day of work tomorrow, and favor me with a night of refreshing rest. Enable me to use the fruits of my labor to please Thee and to help my fellow men. I ask this in the name of Thy Son, who knew the sweat of toil and who shed His blood to earn my sonship with Thee. Amen.

## On Taking a New Position

**1**

Dear Father in heaven, I recognize work as a blessing from Thee and also a duty. I want to serve Thee in my work. I want to provide a comfortable living for myself and my family in keeping with Thy word: "If any provide not for his own, and specially for those of his own house, he hath denied the faith and is worse than an infidel." I want to support Thy kingdom in keeping with Thy word: "Upon the first day of the week let every one of you lay by him in store, as God hath prospered him." And I want to help the poor according to Thy word: "Blessed is he that considereth the poor."

To be better able to serve these purposes, Lord, I have taken a new position. Grant that my new work may be enjoyable for me and that I may be able to serve Thee and my fellow men in richer measure through this change in employment. He whom Thou blessest is blessed indeed. Therefore I pray Thee, crown my action with Thy gracious benediction. Make me faithful in every duty. Give me a kind and loving heart that I may get along well with the new associates in my work. Make me respectful toward my superiors and noble toward those whose work I am to direct. In all my actions help me to show that I love Thee and serve Thee.

When difficulties arise in my work, make me patient and persevering until they are solved. When successes come to me, help me to recognize them as coming from Thee, and keep me humble at all times. Show me how best to use the fruits of my labors in serving mankind and Thee. Keep me faithful in all things until my earthly work is ended and I shall be in heaven with Thee; through Jesus Christ. Amen.

## 2

Lord Jesus, to whom nothing is new or strange, for Thou knowest all things, I ask for Thy gracious guidance as I assume the responsibilities of my new position.

Grant me the grace to be a faithful steward of the talents entrusted by Thy providence to my care. Help me to apply myself in such a way that my work will be fruitful and pleasing to Thee. Give me a sense of honesty and loyalty, and keep me mindful of the accounting I must render Thee for my stewardship.

Above all, give me a true sense of my Christian vocation so that in all things Thou mayest be glorified and that my fellow men with whom I come into contact may discover in me the power of Thy death and resurrection.

Keep me humble in the midst of my successes, cheerful in the face of failure, determined in spite of difficulties, and honest in all my dealings.

Bless my work, and use me in my new position to be a blessing to others. Hear me, Lord Jesus, for Thou art my real Employer, and I am Thy servant. Amen.

*On Receiving a Promotion*

Gracious God, from whom cometh down every good and perfect gift, I come to Thee with thanksgiving and praise for Thy wondrous mercy in granting me this promotion to a higher position. Help me to regard it as a sacred trust from Thee. Enable me to put my time and talents to the best use. Let me look upon my new assignment not merely as a job to be done but as an opportunity for service to mankind and to Thee.

Keep me duly conscious of my stewardship, and make me diligent in the performance of my daily tasks, humble and respectful toward those placed over me, co-operative and helpful toward my co-workers, and patient and understanding toward those in my charge. Lead me to render service "not with eyeservice, as menpleasers, but as the servant of Christ, doing the will of God from the heart." Teach me in the discharge of my calling to do justly, love mercy, and walk humbly before Thee, remembering that One is my Master, even Christ, and that all men are my brethren. And one day enable me to render to Thee a good account of my stewardship; through Jesus Christ. Amen.

*When Going on Vacation*

Lord Jesus Christ, I am grateful for a vacation. I am tired of the hustle and bustle of daily life. I know that it will be good for me to follow Thy example and go "to the other side" for a while, seeking recreation in rest and change.

But I would not go without Thee. I need Thy presence every hour of my vacation. Do Thou keep me close to Thee while I am away from home in strange surroundings. Make me strong to resist all temptations to sin and shame. May Thy Spirit help me to conduct myself as a Christian. Help me to use my vacation wisely that I may be refreshed in body, mind, and spirit.

Send Thy holy angels to protect me on my vacation travels. Amid all the dangers of the crowded highways, and wherever else I may be, keep me safe from harm and danger, and at the close of vacation days bring me safely back home again.

In Thy holy name I both pray and go. **Amen.**


*On Returning from Vacation*

Lord God, heavenly Father, my pleasant vacation days are over. It was good to be away for a little while from tasks of everyday life. I am grateful for the season of relaxation, for the new friends I have made, for the increased appreciation of the wonders of Thy creation.

Go with me, heavenly Father, on my homeward journey, and give me a joyful reunion with my loved ones. Grant me the grace to do the tasks of my calling with renewed zeal, making the most of the talents which Thou hast bestowed on me as a sacred trust. Let me find joy in sharing my blessings with those who are less fortunate and in giving cheerfully for the work my church is doing at home and abroad.

Forgive all that was amiss in thought, word, or deed during my vacation, and in the season of renewed activity help me to walk in the way of Thy Commandments. In Jesus' name. Amen.

*While on Strike*

Dear Father in heaven, I thank Thee for the blessing of work and of daily bread. Let me never forget Thy goodness in providing food and shelter, and grant that I may ever look to Thee for my needs of body and soul.

Owing to disagreements between my labor union and my employer, I am now on strike and out of work. I know Thou lovest all men, and it is Thy will that I love all men as brothers. Therefore help me, my fellow workers, and my employer to overcome all selfishness and pride and to seek a fair solution of our difficulties.

Look with mercy on all who are out of work, and provide for their bodily needs. Give us food, clothing, and shelter, and keep us and our families from suffering and harm.

Protect the property of strikers and employers during the conferences between them. Give our employer a sympathetic understanding of the problems and needs of his workers. Likewise give me and the other workers a proper insight into the problems and resources of our employer, that we may not ask more than is reasonable. Prevent bitterness and strife, and where ungodly strife is present, grant Thy healing and peace. Guide the negotiations toward an early agreement whereby both employer and worker may profit. May fairness and justice prevail for all concerned. And when an agreement is reached and we return to work, grant that all bitterness may be forgotten. Help us all to live and work together in unity of heart and mind.

Give Thy blessing to honest labor everywhere that the needs of mankind may be supplied and that Thy kingdom may flourish; through Jesus Christ. Amen.

*For the Unemployed*

Dear Father in heaven, Giver of all good things, I thank Thee that Thou hast created me and preserved me to this day. Thou knowest my needs and my fears because of my present unemployment. I pray Thee, comfort and strengthen me, and help me to maintain my hope and courage.

It is clear from Thy Word that work is normal and good for man, yet I have not found the work which I need and seek. This situation is hard to understand. Help me, Lord, to surrender wholly to Thee and to look to Thee for the employment which I need.

I pray Thee, Lord, correct what is wrong with me or with the employment situation in general, and give me the opportunity to earn my own bread. Open a door to employment which I do not now see. Keep me from discouragement and bitterness, and help me to put my trust in Thee. Help me to say with a believing heart: "The eyes of all wait upon Thee, O Lord, and Thou givest them their meat in due season. Thou openest Thine hand and satisfiest the desire of every living thing."

In that knowledge and in that faith make me trusting and patient. In the meantime care for me and mine according to Thy promise. I trust Thou wilt do so for the sake of Jesus Christ, my Savior, in whom Thou hast promised to give us all things. Amen.

### *The Businessman*

Heavenly Father, at the beginning of another day I pray Thee, teach me to use acceptably the talents which Thou hast entrusted to my care.

Give me a healthy body and mind that I may be able to meet the responsibilities of my position in life. While making money, preserve me from the love of money. While gaining the temporal, keep me from losing the eternal.

May I always be honest in my business, not only because honesty is the best policy but because it is Thy will. Keep me from being covetous and selfish, and let me deal with those employed by me according to the great commandment, "Thou shalt love thy neighbor as thyself."

Forgive me where I have failed in the past, and with every passing day let me become a more faithful steward of Thy bountiful trust. In Jesus' name I pray. Amen.

## The Laboring Man

Lord Jesus, Thou wast a carpenter's son and dost know the joys and sorrows of a laboring man. Thou dost know the dignity of labor, for Thou didst labor by the sweat of Thy brow and through Thy apostle didst command every man "to work with his hands the thing which is good, that he may have to give to him that needeth." Help me to be faithful in my work, and grant me the grace to work for Thee, my Master. Enable me to be a source of joy to my earthly employer by giving him the best of my service, an honest portion of my time, and a ready willingness to co-operate in the discharge of his requirements. Give my employer a sense of his responsibilities to Thee, and bless him in his position of trust.

Prosper the work of my hands so that my earnings can be put to uses pleasing to Thee. If it be Thy will, keep me in good health, and preserve to me continued employment.

When I fall short of what I ought to be, forgive me, Lord Jesus. Help me in all I do to show that I am Thine and that Thou art my Lord and Master. Enable me to be a good example by my speech and conduct, so that those with whom I work may be drawn to Thee and find the joy which is mine in being Thine. Amen.

*Labor Leaders*

Lord Jesus Christ, who in Thine own city of Nazareth didst labor with Thy hands and thus didst bless our toil, we pray Thee, look with favor upon all skilled and unskilled workers whose efforts supply mankind with the necessities and comforts of life. In particular, lend wisdom and understanding to me and all those who are labor leaders.

Make me increasingly aware of the importance of my role in conducting the activities of my organization according to Christian principles. Help me to establish and maintain high standards of workmanship in our crafts. Teach me to be a faithful leader who will direct my group to render unselfish service, as to Thee, and for the public welfare. Let me bear in mind that we are all members of one great economic body and that the losses of one group adversely affect all the others.

Dispose me to work for industrial peace, harmony, and co-operation. Restrain among us all criminal leadership that strives for selfish gain and glory. Fill me with a sense of honor, decency, and responsibility. Impress upon me that one day I must lay aside my tools to appear before Thy judgment seat, where I must give an account of my activities. May mine be a good accounting; for Jesus' sake. Amen.

*Management*

Lord God, heavenly Father, I recognize the responsibility which Thou hast given me in choosing me to be an employer and a manager of people. I know that every success in my work is from Thee and that my office is a sacred trust which I am to execute for Thee and for the benefit of mankind. I thank Thee for my position of trust and for every blessing on my work which Thou hast given.

I pray Thee, Lord, make me adequate for the duties of my office. Give me the mind of

Thy Son Jesus Christ, who sacrificed that others might profit, who died that others might live, and who always placed the welfare of people above material gain. As I seek to expand business and to increase legitimate profits, keep me honest in all things, and help me to remember that my first service is to Thee. Make me considerate and kind, and show me how to be fair both to my business and to the people who work for me. Increase my ability to work with people, and give me success in helping them to develop to their full capacity. Grant me the patience to deal with them as a Christian should.

At all times, Lord, keep me true to Thee and to Thy Word, and help me to witness to the fact that Thou art my Creator, my Redeemer, and my Comforter. Hear me in Jesus' name. Amen.

*For Guidance in Vocation*

O Lord, heavenly Father, Thou hast promised to watch over Thy children wherever they may be and to guide them in all their ways.

Be Thou my Guide in my work, and help me to work in such a way that Thou wilt be pleased. Give me the wisdom necessary to make the proper decisions in problems which confront me daily.

Above all else, remind me continually by Thy Spirit that Thou hast called me by Thy

Gospel to be Thy child and that it is my business at all times to be a Christian. Grant me a better understanding of my Christian vocation so that all I do in my work may reflect glory upon Thee, my heavenly Father.

Guide me into paths of integrity and honesty for Thy name's sake, lest men mock Thee because of my denial of Thee through hypocrisy and dishonesty. Forgive me when I deny Thee, even as Thou didst forgive Peter when he disclaimed Thee as his Lord.

Help me to use my talents wisely in my work, for I desire to give a good account of my stewardship. Enable me to be a blessing to those with whom and for whom I work, to their joy, and to Thy glory. Amen.

*For Guidance
in the Choice of a Vocation*

Dear God, I thank Thee for a sound body and mind and for all schooling and training in preparation for a vocation. Now the time has come when I must make a choice which will give direction to my life and work. I realize the seriousness of the situation, and I come to Thee for guidance and counsel.

O Lord, give me the proper attitude toward work. Help me always to remember that it is Thy will that I work in a useful vocation, one in which I can serve Thee and my neighbor. Thou hast given me health and talents. I depend on Thee to lead me into some work whereby my talents can best be utilized, in which I will be happy and content, and by which I can make a good living. Help me to think clearly, and open the right opportunity for me. If I cannot immediately find the work I prefer, make me patient and persevering, and help me to serve Thee in whatever work is available.

As I grow in experience and competence, lead me on to greater service and responsibility if it pleases Thee, but keep me ever from conflict with others in order to satisfy my own ambitions. I pray Thee also, show me opportunities to speak for Thee in my daily contact with fellow workers and give me the faith and courage to confess my faith and to lead others to Thee. Grant me the grace of a godly life that I may be a witness for Thee by my daily actions. In all things help me to believe and to do what is right and to be a good workman for Thee; in the name of Jesus. Amen.

*Doctors*

Lord God Eternal, Creator of life and Healer of our souls, Thou hast given to us children of humanity a wonderful and useful body, which we are to make temples of Thy indwelling. To me Thou hast granted the privilege to make special study of the human body, its functions as well as its ailments. Grant that I remember at all times that each patient entrusted to my care is a soul redeemed through Thy Son on Calvary and precious in Thy sight. Give me the needed wisdom to diagnose each case correctly and to prescribe the necessary remedy to heal the body and to ease its pain. Restore to health and useful living the patients entrusted to my care. I need Thy guidance, Thy help, O Lord, and the will to meet my responsibilities. Help me to conquer all self-seeking, all irritations, all impatience. Make me cheerful. Help me by my word and action to fill the hearts of my patients with hope, confidence, and courage. Above all, let me realize day after day that I am dependent upon Thee as my God. May I at all times bear testimony of my faith and my loyalty to Jesus, my Savior and the Great Physician of our souls. Amen.

*Nurses*

Almighty God, who dost give and maintain life, I thank Thee for having fitted me for the art of relieving suffering and lessening pain. May I always be faithful to my noble profession.

Give me strength for each day's duties. Make me brave, patient, kind, and understanding. Help me to ease the pain of those entrusted to my care and to bring rest to troubled hearts. In loyal service and devoted care let me reflect Thy boundless love.

In my ministrations to the physical needs of others, may I also be granted the privilege of winning souls for Thee, realizing that people on their sickbed yearn not only for strength of body but also for peace of mind. Let me, O gracious Lord, be one of Thy instruments in accomplishing Thy purposes.

Be near me always to guide me, to help me, and to use me in the ministry to the sick and suffering; for Jesus' sake. Amen.

*Workers in Hospitals and Nursing Homes*

Lord Jesus, Thou art the heavenly Physician who art able to give health to the body, wholesomeness to the mind, and peace to the soul.

Conduct Thy ministry of mercy in all the hospitals and nursing homes of our land, and grant Thy healing to the distressed.

Give me patience and wisdom as I minister to the needy, and grant me a special measure of love and understanding toward those who are frightened and in pain.

Walk down the corridors of our hospital, and enter every room with Thy tender mercy and healing care. Use me to bring hope and courage to the lonely and the discouraged. Give me opportunities to speak a word for Thee and Thy forgiving grace, and then grant me the grace to speak in a winsome way.

Show Thyself as the Savior especially to the dying, so that at their departing they may inherit the eternal joys and rest of their heavenly home.

Send Thy holy angels to watch over us, and grant to all who work here the wisdom each one needs for his (her) appointed task. When I become weary in serving others, keep me from becoming tired of serving. But remind me by Thy Spirit that Thou didst not come to be served but to serve, and to give Thy life a ransom for many. Hear me, O Lord Jesus, for Thy name's sake. Amen.

*Lawyers*

Heavenly Father, I thank Thee that Thou hast called me into the honored profession of law, where I have the opportunity to be of special service to Thee and to my fellow men. Keep me worthy, I pray, of the sacred trust committed to my care.

May I always be aware that the authority of the law has been ordained by Thee. Help me in the practice of my profession to uphold the laws of our country and of this state. Make me desirous to have truth and righteousness prevail at all times. May any counsel I give to those who come to me for advice be in accord with the letter and spirit of our laws and never contrary to Thy Word.

If Thou shouldest grant me success and honor in my profession, I pray Thee to keep me humble and generous. May my conduct in both my personal and professional life always redound to Thy glory. In Jesus' name. Amen.

*State Officials*

Gracious God, heavenly Father, Thou hast revealed in Thy Word that rule and authority in government are in keeping with Thy divine order. Keep me mindful, I pray Thee, of the sacred trust which Thou hast committed to my care by using me, as an officer of the state, to carry out Thy plans.

Give me wisdom and understanding that I may perform the duties of my office for the good of my fellow citizens. Grant me Thy grace that I may never use my office to enrich myself nor to serve selfish interests.

Hear Thou my prayer, and lead me in the paths of righteousness in which Thou wouldst have me walk, for the good of our state and for Thy name's sake. In Jesus' name. Amen.

*City Officials*

Except Thou, Lord Omnipotent, keep the city, the wickedness and cunning of sinful men will destroy us. Therefore I come to Thee, placing into Thy hands the needs of our city, beseeching Thee to give wisdom and ability, sane judgment, and uprightness of purpose to those who govern us. I know, Lord, that the task is difficult, the duties are many, and the responsibilities heavy. I pray for them that Thou wouldst uphold them with Thy might, that crime and lawlessness be hindered and righteousness and integrity prevail.

Make me a law-abiding citizen and one who will seek the welfare of the community. Above all, grant that more people within the boundaries of our city will accept Jesus as their Savior and serve Him with faithfulness and untiring zeal. Make ours a truly Christian community, and give us officials who will dedicate themselves wholeheartedly to Thee and to their tasks and assignments. Then Thine is the glory and the praise through endless days. In Jesus' name. Amen.

*Teachers*

**1**

Heavenly Father, Thou hast called me into a vocation of great responsibility as a teacher of growing boys and girls. Keep me aware of my obligation to help prepare them for their place in life and to teach them to be mindful of their duties to God and man.

I pray Thee, give me patience and kindness, wisdom and understanding, in dealing with the children entrusted to my care. Prevent me from saying and doing anything in the classroom that would offend "one of these little ones."

Help me so to live in our community that both parents and children may see that Jesus Christ lives in me and I in Him.

Bless me and the children today and always. Amen.

2

O Lord Jesus, Thou art the Teacher sent from God, and Thou art the Wisdom which to know is forgiveness and life and salvation. Thou art the Truth, and to know Thee is to know the Father, who spared Thee not, but gave Thee up for us all.

Help me to be a teacher such as Thou lovest. Give me the right kind of love for each one of Thy children entrusted to my care, that my love will be a true reflection of the love which Thou hast for every individual. Keep me mindful that Thou hast created my pupils and hast given them different talents, all of which are intended to glorify Thee.

Keep me from becoming impatient and fretful. Give me enough success to be encouraged and enough reversals to be kept humble. Enable me to be a loyal co-worker toward those associated with me, and bless their work as well as mine.

Give the parents of my pupils a keen sense of their divinely entrusted responsibilities, and help me to assist them in the training of the young, that in all things Thou mayest be glorified.

Grant me the grace to be a godly example of Christian piety, and use me to be a blessing to those entrusted to me. Hear me for Thy mercy's sake. Amen.

*Technicians*

Heavenly Father, Thou hast revealed Thy wisdom and glory in the universe and entrusted to us mortals the "dominion" or power "over the fish of the sea, and over the fowl of the air, and over every living thing that moveth upon the earth." What a privilege! What a responsibility, Lord! To me Thou hast opened opportunities and insight into the marvels of Thy creation. Grant me the grace to remember at all times that Thou art the Creator of all things visible and invisible and that all that I discover, create, and formulate is made possible by Thy gracious hand. In Thy goodness give me the wisdom and the will to use all my abilities to make the world in which I live a better and more useful world, that all the discoveries and inventions be used for the good of humanity.

Above all, grant that I be ever mindful that all that I am and all ability I possess comes from Thee, who hast given me more than life, yes, also a soul redeemed through Thy Son Jesus Christ. Keep me faithful to Him and steadfast to the church and its saving Gospel. This I ask in His name. Amen.

*Scientists*

Almighty God, Creator of all, whose glory the heavens declare and whose handiwork the firmament reveals, Thou didst provide this marvelous world in which I live with definite, unchangeable laws which man can learn and use for his benefit.

I ask Thee to bless my studies and research to advance the welfare of mankind. Keep me from perverting the forces of Thy creation to the destruction of humanity. Preserve in me a spirit of dedication to my cause that I may help lead the world to the fullest possible use of the material blessings Thou hast created for its enjoyment. As I labor with my instruments and study my test tubes, may I see in all that I do the glories of Thy marvelous creation and thereby be led to recognize Thee as the only true God. Grant that my studies of natural forces may strengthen my faith in the truths of Holy Scripture. Give me the guidance of Thy Spirit that I may become more familiar with the revelation that far exceeds the results of scientific research, and may discover the greatest truth ever unfolded to mankind — that Thy Son came into this world to redeem and to save sinners. Cause me to accept this truth and ever to hold fast to Christ as my personal Savior in a living faith, for His name's and my soul's sake. Amen.


*Farmers*

Lord God, heavenly Father, the earth is Thine, and the cattle of a thousand hills are Thine. Thou art the Source of life which created this world with its rich resources.

Help me to be a good caretaker of the land entrusted to my care. Preserve me from forgetting Thy ownership and my stewardship, lest I become proud and forget Thee, or lest I become careless and waste what is Thine. Fill my heart with gratitude for the yield of the land and the fruits of my labors.

If it be Thy will, grant me bountiful harvests so that I may bountifully praise Thee and bountifully share these blessings for the spreading of Thy saving Gospel. Grant rain in due season, and favor us with good weather. Ward off any pestilence and calamity which may destroy what Thou hast created. If Thou dost see fit to afflict me with failure, keep me humble and penitent, and guard me against complaining and dishonoring Thee.

I thank Thee for Thy past blessings upon my labor. Without Thee I can do nothing. In everything Thou must give the increase. Thou hast been good and gracious, heavenly Father, and I ask Thee, for Jesus' sake, to continue to be merciful to me and to bless me. Amen.

## *Of a Handicapped Child of God*

Heavenly Father, Thou art the Refuge and Strength of all who put their trust in Thee. Thou art a very present Help in trouble, and dost supply grace for every time of need.

Teach me by Thy Holy Spirit to glory in my infirmities and to discover the meaning of Thy gracious promise: "My grace is sufficient for thee, for My strength is made perfect in weakness." Help me to discover Thy strength when I am weak, that I may with fullness of heart praise Thee for Thy mighty care.

When I am tempted to moodiness and despair because of my affliction, when the devil taunts me and tells me that Thou dost not love me, when others are thoughtless and unsympathetic, give me, dear Father in heaven, a clear vision of the Cross of Thy dear Son. Show me the bitterness of His suffering in my behalf, the agony of His crucifixion endured for my redemption, and the power of His resurrection for my deliverance from sin and death and hell.

Show me the advantages of my handicap and the blessings which are mine because of it. Especially do I praise Thee for the kindness of my loved ones, the thoughtfulness of my friends, and the opportunities I have to reflect the love which Thou hast shown me in Christ Jesus, my Lord. Amen.

*Prayers Pertaining to National and International Life*

*For Peace*

Almighty God, Thou Lord of concord and peace, who dost set the limits and boundaries of the nations and dost mark the paths of history in Thy wisdom, justice, and goodness, cause all strife and misunderstanding to cease, and grant peace to our nation. We all are the children of Thy creation and of Thy love, and Thou hast sent Christ Jesus into this world of sin and wickedness to redeem each one of us living on the earth. Thou hast offered to all of us the Gospel of forgiveness and reconciling peace through the precious blood of Thy dear Son.

Grant all of us the grace to accept Thy terms of reconciliation, and let me, too, enjoy the forgiveness of all my sin. I ask Thee, because of Thy pardon to us, to make us forgiving, thoughtful, and considerate of one another. Grant that we of this generation may live side by side in quietness and peace, recognizing that each one of us has rights and privileges given us of

Thee, in Thy goodness of heart. Teach me to look upon others as fellow redeemed and permit them to enjoy those blessings that I want as my own.

Make our nation a righteous nation and us citizens a law-abiding and upright people. Grant health and strength and wisdom to those in authority, especially to our President, and prevent godless and wicked men from corrupting our land. From day to day grant me the grace to live peaceably with those in my community, at work, at the church, and with the associates of my leisure hours, that my conduct and speech may give honor to Thee and Thy Son Jesus Christ, my Savior. Amen.

*For Government*

Almighty God, our Help in ages past, our Hope for years to come, of whom is all rule and authority in the world, I come before Thee with a prayer for our government. I am grateful for the good government which Thou hast ordained to rule in our land. Thou hast dealt favorably with our country and our people. Bless, I implore Thee, all who are in authority in our land with wisdom and understanding, with love for righteousness and peace, that under their leadership our country may continue to enjoy Thy grace and favor.

Help me, by Thy Spirit, as a good citizen to render to our government the things which belong to the government and not to forget that I must render to Thee, my God, what belongs to Thee. May Thy name be hallowed! For Jesus' sake. Amen.

*For the President of the United States*

Almighty God, Ruler of the nations, regard with favor Thy servant, the President of the United States. Grant him health of body and mind; make him strong to bear the burdens of his high office. Give him wisdom and understanding, that under his leadership our nation may be directed in the ways of righteousness and peace.

Teach me and all Christian citizens to realize that rule and authority also in our country are of Thee and that our President is Thy minister in the administration of his office. Keep us mindful of our obligation to support our President with fervent prayer and with ready obedience to the laws of our country.

Bless our President, I pray Thee, and make him a blessing to our people, to the glory of Thy holy name. For Jesus' sake. Amen.

*For the Nation*

Heavenly Father, Ruler of nations, I thank Thee for the countless undeserved blessings which Thou hast showered on our country. Individually and as a nation we have sinned often and grievously, and I pray Thee, mercifully forgive our many transgressions. Endow the leaders of our country with wisdom from on high. Cause them to rule in Thy fear and according to Thy will, that we may lead a quiet and peaceable life in all godliness and honesty and that our nation and its people may prosper both spiritually and temporally.

Hold Thy protecting hand over our nation, over me and mine, and over all Thy children. Preserve our priceless religious liberty to us, and keep all believers faithful to Thee. Bring a great salvation to pass, and turn the hearts of multitudes of unbelievers to accept the peace and comfort which only the faith in their Savior Jesus Christ can bring them.

Give us faith instead of unbelief, courage instead of fear, love instead of hate, peace instead of quarrels and war, and righteousness instead of sin everywhere and in everything. We have indeed deserved nothing but punishment for our sins, but in Thy great mercy be gracious to us, bless us, and hear our prayer for Jesus' sake. Amen.

## For the City

O Lord, our God, who art a God of order and justice and art pleased when men govern and are governed according to Thy will, I beseech Thee, in the name of Jesus Christ, to bless this city and its inhabitants.

Bestow Thy guidance upon all who are in authority. Keep them mindful of their sacred trust in public office, and grant them wisdom for their difficult tasks. Preserve to them a sense of honesty and decency, a spirit of humility and service, and a sensitivity to the needs of the entire citizenry.

Give to all who live here a grateful heart for the advantages we enjoy, ready obedience to our laws, and a profound concern for the rights and privileges of every citizen. Help me to be a light of the world and a salt of the earth in my community, and a blessing to my neighbors.

Protect our city from all calamities and epidemics, and shield us especially from those temptations which could corrupt our officials and cause our citizens to despise Thee, who art Ruler of all.

Bless the preaching of Thy Gospel in our community so that more who live in our city may find their way to the eternal city which hath foundations, whose Builder Thou art and which Thou hast prepared for them that love Thee. Amen.

## For Friendship Among the Nations

O Father of all mankind, who at the birth of Thy Son didst send Thy holy angels to proclaim good will toward men, foster and promote friendship among the nations of the earth. Impress on all men everywhere, regardless of color, race, or national origin, that they are the children of Thy creation, and keep them mindful of their common humanity.

Preside in the councils of world leaders to adjust in friendly fashion all differences that separate nations. Let the love which prompted Thy Son to give His life for our redemption take root in the hearts of those who are charged with the direction of national affairs. Make them realize that they owe a responsibility not only to their own people but also — and above all — to Thee as the Ruler of nations to conduct international relations peaceably as much as lies within their power, for the common welfare.

Bless all efforts to promote friendship and understanding among nations. Enable men everywhere to remove from their thoughts and actions every trace of national pride and selfishness and to extend the hand of welcome and fellowship to foreigners. Cause us to recognize our own faults and shortcomings, and do Thou establish Thy will among the nations of the earth. Bring this to pass, we pray, for Jesus' sake. Amen.

## For Better Understanding Among the Nations

O Father of mankind and Ruler of nations, who wouldst have all men to dwell together in peace and unity, raise up, we ask Thee, leaders in every land who will choose peace instead of war and direct their people in pathways of friendship and understanding toward all men.

Help us all in our respective places to seek justice, to cultivate righteousness, and to walk humbly before Thee. Remove all pride from our hearts. Give us understanding minds so that, regardless of race or nationality, color or station in life, we may realize that we are all of the same flesh and blood, Thy common creation.

Restrain the efforts of those who would sow seeds of hatred and ill will among nations. Bless all efforts for peace. Direct the course of this world that Thy will may be done and Thy kingdom come. Cause quiet and order to prevail everywhere, that the message of Thy Gospel may without any obstacle or hindrance be carried to the far corners of the earth; for the sake of Him who died and rose again that we might live forever. Amen.

## For Washington's Birthday

Almighty God, Lord of the nations, today we commemorate the birthday of him whom we honor as the first President of our country.

I thank and praise Thee for the God-fearing men who served our nation in the critical days of her founding. I thank Thee especially for the wise leadership of George Washington; I am grateful for the inspiration of his confession that "no people can be bound to acknowledge and adore the Invisible Hand which conducts the affairs of men more than those of the United States."

While I am grateful today for all that George Washington and other great presidents have done for the good of our country, I want to acknowledge that it was Thy goodness, O God, that has made and kept us a great nation these many years. Teach me and my fellow citizens to remember that "except the Lord build the house, they labor in vain that build it." Forbid that the Christian people of our country should ever forget Thee, lest we lose Thy favor. In Jesus' name. Amen.


*For Memorial Day*

Almighty and eternal God, Ruler of individuals and of nations, I bring my thanks to Thee this Memorial Day for all the blessings which Thou hast showered on our nation. Prosperity has reigned within our borders, and enemies have not been able to subdue us, because Thou hast graciously held Thy protecting hand over us. Help me to know and to acknowledge that freedom, prosperity, and other blessings come from Thee, and make me thankful.

I confess, Lord, that Thy blessings are entirely undeserved. Irreverence, lust, theft, murder, and sins and crimes of every description are the shame of our privileged country, and with others I can only bow before Thee in shame. Merciful Father, forgive our personal sins and our national sins for Jesus' sake. Enlighten us by Thy Word. Make us upright citizens of our dear country and worthy members of the community in which we live. Move us to bow under authority, first under Thine, and then under the authority of our government. Give us and all the countries of the world a lasting peace, and teach us to live together as befits Thy children. Bring about a mighty Christian revival, and turn to Thee the hearts of millions who now live in unbelief.

As my memories go back to those who have died to preserve our liberties, make me grateful and humble. Give me the determination to do all in my power to safeguard our freedom. Make me diligent in prayer for my country, guide and lead those in authority with Thy sure counsel, and give power to all Christian witness that not only the Christians of today but also many others may be brought to eternal life through Thee; for Jesus' sake. Amen.

*For Dominion Day*

Lord of the nations, who settest the limit to the powers of man and lettest nations run their appointed course, on this Dominion Day I praise Thee, most holy God, that Thou hast established and preserved this Dominion in the free world of our day. Ours has been a glorious liberty and ours a wonderful country to live in, a vast and prosperous homeland extending from the Atlantic to the Pacific and to the regions of the frozen North.

I beseech Thee, Lord of heaven and earth, protect us from war and disaster, from sorrow and tears, from atomic destruction. Give us wise leaders, unselfish men, who at all times place the welfare of the people first. Continue to let us live at peace with the United States and show the nations of the world that two great governments can live side by side without fear, suspicion, and envy and without border fortifications. Preserve this splendid and friendly relationship and good will between us.

On this day, then, accept my thanks as I make known my appreciation to all for the privilege of being permitted to live in this good and blessed land. Continue to be with us as Thou hast been in the past, through Jesus Christ, my Savior and Lord. Amen.

## For Independence Day

O God, our Help in ages past, our Hope for years to come, I give Thee grateful thanks on this anniversary of the signing of the Declaration of Independence for the priceless blessings of liberty that with Thy help were won for me by my forefathers. Stir up within me, I pray Thee, a new appreciation of the life, liberty, and pursuit of happiness I enjoy in this land of the free, and a greater readiness to serve my nation with my talents. Teach me, above all, to treasure that precious freedom of conscience and worship, without which other liberties would not long survive. May I never contribute to the loss of these dearly won blessings by my own selfishness, ambition, or indifference.

Teach me furthermore, O Lord, that the enjoyment of freedom brings with it also the responsibility to serve. To that end make me willing to respect the laws of my country, to serve my fellow citizens well in any office of trust to which I may be elected, to exercise faithfully my privilege to vote, and to give my loyal support to all public institutions.

Bless all those in authority. Give wisdom and faithfulness to those in positions of leadership. Preserve them from becoming the prey of selfish pressure groups, and give them willingness to serve the interests of the public.

Grant enduring peace to our country and its institutions, so that Thy Gospel may be able without hindrance to turn the hearts of all from the bondage of sin to the freedom won by the blood of our precious Redeemer, in whose name and for whose sake we ask this. Amen.

*For Labor Day*

Lord Jesus, who as a youth didst work in Joseph's carpenter shop, making Thyself useful, help me to perform my assigned tasks with faithfulness and with cheerful heart. Bless Thou management and labor. May all who must work together in office and shop be mindful of the Golden Rule which Thou hast given to mankind, and, following Thy directions, render the best possible service one to another. May we all seek each other's good, be thoughtful, helpful, and courteous.

Prosper the nation, that all may find employment and none suffer from want. To us who have aplenty give Thou the grace to share with those who are unable to work because of sickness and feebleness of body. Above all, grant that all people of the world, burdened with sin, may come to Thee and Thy Cross to find healing and salvation. I ask this of Thee, my Savior and my Lord, who hast come into the world to seek and to save those who are lost. Amen.

## For Veterans' Day

Lord Jesus, the Captain of my soul, who didst know the pain of battle with the old evil Foe in order to secure my redemption, grant me a grateful heart for the freedoms I enjoy through Thy grace and mercy.

Help me to treasure my spiritual freedom from sin, death, and the devil, and open Thou my lips continually to praise Thee for my liberty in Thee.

Teach me to be thankful for my liberties in this blessed land, which were won and preserved for me by the sacrifices of my countrymen in times past. Help me to honor their memory by a conscientious and loyal citizenship and a readiness to defend the rights of free men everywhere.

Grant Thy comfort to families who this day remember with sorrow the death of one who gave his life for our country. Sustain those veterans who are confined to hospitals throughout our land, who bear the scars of war, so that I might enjoy the wholesomeness of peace and freedom.

Preserve me from forgetfulness of the heroes of the past, lest I become a coward in the face of the future. Grant the gift of peace to our land and to the world, so that Thy Gospel may have free course and more men everywhere may march under Thy lordship beneath the banner of Thy Cross. Amen.

*For the Opening of Congress*

At the opening of a new session of Congress, I pray Thee, heavenly Father, to take into Thy gracious care all members of the Senate and of the House of Representatives, the presiding officers, and all other officials. Endow them with a high sense of responsibility of the office to which they have been elected. Make them immune to the temptations of selfish interests. Fill them with knowledge and wisdom, that the resolutions adopted and the laws enacted may meet Thy standards and be for the good of our people.

Keep me and my fellow citizens from unfair criticism and faultfinding. Help us rather, O God, at the opening of this new session to render to the members of Congress the honor and respect which is proper and to support them with our prayers and our good will.

Bless our country, bless our government, bless our people, and make our nation a blessing to the people of the world. For Jesus' sake. Amen.

*During Wartime*

Lord Jesus Christ, Thou Prince of Peace, who hatest wars, in which men slay their own brothers and destroy those things which Thou hast given us to enjoy, forgive us for wars and fightings among us and for the lust of our flesh that begets them.

O Thou who makest wars to cease unto the ends of the earth, bring a speedy end to this reign of destruction and terror. Restore men to sanity so that they may see the insanity of war and avoid it as a sore plague of mankind and an offense to Thy holy majesty.

Turn the hearts of our enemies to peace, and crush in Thy power all those who would destroy the creatures whom Thou hast made to honor Thee.

Plow deep into the souls of men everywhere, that the precious seed of Thy Gospel may take root and bear the fruits of faith and love, that men everywhere may find their peace in Thee.

Keep me in the true faith, that whether I live or whether I die I may be Thine and Thou mayest be mine to adore and to praise forever as the Lamb slain for my sins from before the foundation of the world.

Abide with me, Lord Jesus, that I may ever abide in Thee and forever with Thee. Amen.

*Men and Women
in the Armed Services*

Merciful Father in heaven, I thank Thee for Thy presence and for the comforting assurance of Thy love and guidance; for the salvation in Jesus Christ; for the consolation of Thy Word; for my praying relatives and friends both near and far; for Thy protection in danger and temptation.

Lord, I pray Thee, go with me day by day and from task to task. Forgive my sins for Jesus' sake, and strengthen my faith. Help me to serve my country ably and loyally, and, above all, keep me faithful to my Lord and Savior Jesus Christ. Keep me loyal also to relatives and friends, and keep them in Thy loving care until I return to them. Strengthen me in the conviction that my service in the Armed Forces is a service to my country and to Thee. Help me to overcome every sin and temptation, and give me the necessary strength for a holy, reverent, chaste, and honest life in word and deed.

Make me an example to my fellow Christians and to unbelievers alike. Give me the courage to confess Thy holy name and to witness for Thee as I have opportunity. Strengthen my love for the whole cause of the Christian Church, and help me to work and to sacrifice that Thy name may be glorified. Grant graciously that my whole life may be a service to Thee; in the name of Jesus Christ. Amen.

*During Unfavorable Weather*

Lord God, who givest rain and sunshine, summer and winter, cold and heat in due season, we ask Thee in these days of unfavorable weather to uphold us and provide for the needs of man and beast. As Thy chastening hand tries our patience and tests our faith and reliance on Thee, we ask Thee to forgive our many sins of ingratitude. So often have we forgotten to thank Thee for Thy goodness and acknowledge Thy many mercies. We confess that we have not at all times sought Thee to bless us and our daily work. Forgive us, and teach us to look up to Thee, each day, appreciative of rain and sunshine, warmth and cold, seedtime and harvest, as Thou in Thy wisdom through all kinds of weather conditions dost feed us all.

In Thy mercy give us weather which is favorable to our needs as a nation and people. Protect us against storms and cold, against hunger and want. Pour out Thy blessings and benedictions on us, and make us grateful and thankful for all that we receive from Thy bountiful hand. Then Thine shall be the praise and the glory through Jesus, Thy Son and our Redeemer and Friend. Amen.

*For Rain*

Almighty God, who controllest the wind and the waves, we come to Thee asking for rain. At such a time as this we realize particularly that we are small and sinful and that Thou art great and good. But Thou hast promised to take care of Thy children, and we know that Thy promises are sure. Therefore, through the atoning death of our blessed Savior, which has made us Thy beloved children, we are bold to bring also our present request to Thee. O Lord of all, open the windows of heaven and send Thy showers of blessing.

We have prepared the soil and have planted the seed. But if Thou dost not send sunshine and rain, all our efforts are in vain. Be pleased, therefore, to hear our petitions, and send us refreshing rain, that the parched land may be moistened and the thirst of Thy creatures quenched.

O Thou who satisfiest the desire of every living thing, we praise and glorify Thy name and proclaim Thy goodness among our fellow men. Grant our request, if it be Thy will, for Jesus' sake. Amen.


*In Days of Drought*

God of mercy and of truth, we come to Thee chastened and penitent, and we pray Thee, look not on our sins, and do not punish us in Thy displeasure. The heat and the drought have taken their toll; the fruits of the field languish for lack of rain. Many hearts are weary and fearful. We know we have deserved none of the good things which Thou hast given us, and we do not deserve an answer to our prayers. But in Thy mercy Thou hast promised to send the early and the latter rains and to water the earth that it may bring forth fruit in due season. Therefore we appeal to Thy mercy and to Thy promise.

Refresh the drooping fields with rain as in the days of Elijah. Spare the beautiful trees of Thy creation, revive the grass and the flowers, and help us to regard them all as gifts of Thy love and as evidences of Thy gracious, almighty power. Give us and all Thy creatures the food which we need. Help those who have been impoverished by the drought. Open the hearts of the fortunate toward the unfortunate. Remind us that we depend on Thee, and draw us and all mankind closer together in peace and in good works.

Help us to walk in Thy Commandments and to turn to Thee in every need. Refresh and renew our bodies and minds that we may rejoice in Thee. In prosperity or adversity help us to sing praises to Thee; for the sake of Jesus Christ, our Lord and Savior. Amen.

*Prayers in Time of Sickness*

*Before an Operation*

As I face this operation, gracious Father in Christ, I come to Thee with my fears and misgivings and ask Thee to put into my heart the needed courage to face the day with confidence because of Thy goodness and protection. Thou dost not slumber nor sleep while I am in a deep sleep. Let this be an assurance to me that I need not worry nor be afraid. Relax my nerves, put my mind at ease, and graciously forgive me all my sins.

Give to the surgeon a steady hand and the necessary understanding to do his task with ease and with perfection. Give to my family the reassuring faith that Thou art with us, the Keeper of my body and the Lover of my soul. Calm their troubled spirit during the coming hours of my operation. Into Thy precious hands I entrust my well-being for time and eternity. This I ask in the name of my Lord and Savior Jesus Christ. Amen.

*After an Operation*

My grateful heart praises Thee, heavenly Father, that Thou hast safely seen me through this operation. I know all went well because Thou didst watch over me. During the hours and the days which lie ahead ease my distress and pain, and heal me. Give me the needed patience, the necessary endurance, and continued confidence that Thy goodness and love will uphold me.

Grant that all service which the nurses give to me will hasten my recovery, and then bring me safely home, completely healed. Give me restful days, and bless me this night with refreshing sleep. Let me enjoy Thy peace through the forgiveness of all my sin, for which Christ paid in full on the cross. Continue to abide with me now and always. Amen.


*Prayers for the Sickroom*

1

Lord Jesus Christ, Thou wast never too busy to spend time with the sick and those afflicted with pain. I ask Thee to continue to show mercy to me in my illness and to comfort me with Thy presence.

Give me a repentant faith in Thee, for my illness reminds me that I have sinned against

Thee. Wash my sins away in Thy blood, and strengthen my faith in Thy promises of perfect pardon.

Sustain me in my moments of discouragement. Grant relief from my pain if it will be for my good. Bless those who wait on me, and help me to make their task lighter by a spirit of cheerful appreciation for their kindness.

Grant healing in Thy good time, O Lord. Bless me with patience, and help me to wait on Thee for a release from my sickness. Keep me from complaining. Watch over the loved ones from whom I am separated, and preserve them in true faith and good health.

I wait on Thee, Lord Jesus, and in Thy Word do I hope. Amen.

2

O Lord Christ, who art the Physician of men's bodies and souls, who forgivest all our iniquities and healest all our diseases, I ask Thee to step into my sickroom and deal with me according to Thy wisdom and mercy.

Help me to see myself as I really am, a sinner deserving Thy wrath and punishment, yet Thy disciple and heir of Thy forgiveness and salvation. Keep on reminding me by Thy Spirit of Thy great love for me, for I am plagued frequently by disturbing doubts and fears. Remove from me the worries concerning the expenses caused by my sickness and the discomfort I am causing others by my illness. Reassure me that Thou wilt provide for all my needs according to the riches of Thy grace.

Keep me from feeling sorry for myself, but give me rather true sorrow over my sin and a lively and persevering hope in Thy mercy. Grant me the grace to be grateful to those who wait on me and demonstrate their love for me through their service. Restore me to health, if it be Thy will, when it is Thy will. I commit myself, my body and soul, into Thy keeping.

I trust Thee, Lord Jesus, and I know I can rely on Thee to do what is best for me. Amen.

## 3

Almighty God, Author of life and health, I come before Thee asking that Thou wouldst help me in my bodily need. In Thy wise providence Thou hast laid me upon this bed of illness and pain. Be merciful to me, O Lord, and, if it be Thy will, give me relief from my suffering. Bless the efforts of my physician to restore me to health. Grant me steady improvement until I am entirely well again. Preserve me from relapses or complications, and make my recovery swift and complete.

Meanwhile give me patience to await Thy deliverance. And if it should be Thy will that I linger on my sickbed, grant me the confidence that Thou doest all things well. When Thy will is accomplished in me, deliver me from this cross which Thou hast laid upon me.

Through this experience draw me closer to Thee. Watch over my bed. Preserve me from temptation by the Evil One. Grant me courage to look into the future unafraid, knowing that Thou art with me and that I have no cause to fear.

Help me by this experience to grow more Christlike in my attitudes, and finally by Thy mercy bring me to everlasting glory. Grant this for Jesus' sake. Amen.

## 4

Dear heavenly Father, in my weakness I come to Thee asking for help. I need Thee so much, and I realize how helpless I am without Thee. I ask Thee to give me strength for today, and I will not worry about tomorrow.

My physical illness reminds me of my spiritual illness. Thou art also the Physician of my soul. Grant me the peace of mind that comes from sins forgiven and the joy of knowing Thee as that Friend that sticketh closer than a brother.

If I recover from this affliction, help me to serve my fellow men and to glorify Thee. Keep before me the blessed example of Thy beloved Son, who went about doing good.

Make me patient and grateful. Bless the doctors, the nurses, and all who are taking care of me. Watch over my loved ones while I am absent from them. Stay close beside me always, and finally take me home to Thee in heaven. In Jesus' name I ask this. Amen.

## 5

I thank Thee, gracious God, for Thy comforting word, "Call upon Me in the day of trouble; I will deliver thee, and thou shalt glorify Me." I confess that I am unworthy to appear in Thy presence, for I have sinned much and have indeed deserved nothing but punishment. But Thou art a gracious God who, for the sake of Jesus Christ, hast forgiven me my trespasses and dost remember them no more.

So I accept Thy invitation to call upon Thee in this day of trouble; I pray Thee to deliver me from the sickness of my body. I would not prescribe to Thee how and when deliverance should come, for Thou knowest what is best for me.

Answer my prayer, dear Lord, by sending me that deliverance which is in keeping with Thy gracious plans for my life. I promise to glorify Thee with all that I am and have. In Jesus' precious name. Amen.

## 6

Lord Jesus Christ, who art the Savior of my soul, I pray Thee, be the Savior also of my body. If it be Thy will, make me well again. I know that Thy miracle-working power is not shortened and that Thou canst heal my sick body even though all earthly helpers should fail. As Thou in Gethsemane didst leave everything to the will of Thy heavenly Father, so I would leave everything to Thee; for Thy will, not mine, is best.

Bless those who wait on me in the sickroom, the doctors, the nurses, and all others. Bless those who are praying for me. Reward them all according to Thy loving-kindness. Hear my prayer, Lord Jesus. Amen.

## 7

Divine and gracious Savior, I beseech Thee to take full possession of my heart and life. Let me know that each moment of this day Thou art with me, protecting me with Thy grace and preserving me through Thy love. Help me to overcome the discouragements which are coming into my day, and ease my pain. Remove from my heart all self-pity, take all resentment from my mind, and let me live trustingly one day at a time as I lean on Thee. Give me a hopeful outlook for this day, and remove all irritation from the coming night. Let my patience increase as I ponder upon Thy mercies, precious Savior. Amen.

## 8

I lift up mine eyes to Thee, O Lord, my Refuge and Strength. Trusting in Thy promises, I know that Thou wilt not fail me in this hour of trouble and that Thou wilt give me the strength I need and the help which is necessary. Today let Thy mercies again override all my worries. Keep me calm, untroubled, unalarmed. Ease my pain, and let Thy divine forgiveness speak peace to my soul through Jesus Christ, my Lord. Fill me with the grace of cheerfulness and patience, hope and confidence.

Bless our household with a greater faith and a larger hopefulness as we carry on from day to day in this trouble and in my illness. Remove from my heart all fears and misgivings. Give me a quiet and restful day and a peaceful night of sleep. I ask this in Jesus' name. Amen.

## 9

Heavenly and gracious Father in Christ Jesus, as I come to Thy throne of grace and mercy, fulfill Thy promise to be with me and to deliver me out of all my distresses and pain. I need encouragement and strength, which can come only from Thy almighty hand. Enable me to entrust myself completely to Thy care, giving me hope and patience, courage and confidence.

In Thy loving-kindness forgive me all my sin. Put my mind completely at ease because I know that I have Thee as heavenly Father, and relax my nerves because I can rely upon Thee to watch over me every hour of the day. Bless those who take care of me, and let Thy healing hand bring about a speedy recovery.

Purify my heart, uplift me by Thy Spirit, and let me live trustingly in Thy presence. Let the continued blessings of my Savior comfort me as I remember that through Him I am a child of Thy household and coheir of life eternal. Give me a quiet day, and bless me this night with refreshing sleep as I receive Thy benediction through Jesus Christ, the Shepherd of my soul and the closest Friend of my life. Amen.

## 10

"Save me, O God; for the waters are come in unto my soul. I sink in deep mire, where there is no standing; I am come into deep waters, where the floods overflow me. I am weary of my crying; my throat is dried; mine eyes fail while I wait for my God. . . . O God, Thou knowest my foolishness, and my sins are not hid from Thee. . . . But as for me, my prayer is unto Thee, O Lord, in an acceptable time. O God, in the multitude of Thy mercy hear me, in the truth of Thy salvation. . . . Hear me, O Lord; for Thy loving-kindness is good; turn unto me according to the multitude of Thy tender mercies. And hide not Thy face from Thy servant, for I am in trouble; hear me speedily. Draw nigh unto my soul, and redeem it. Deliver me." Amen. (Selected from Psalm 69.)

## 11

Lord Jesus, Strength of the weary and a very present Help to all who are in distress, I come to Thee with all my burdens and sins. Send Thy divine cleansing and healing into my life. Safely see me through the troubles and pains of the day. Take all sinful thoughts and worries out of my heart, and let me find peace in Thee. Lead me daily to Calvary to behold Thy boundless love, O gracious Savior.

Fill my soul with the joy of forgiveness and the hope of everlasting life. Let not the sufferings and the cares of today make me despondent, but teach me to believe that Thy abiding presence will uphold me from hour to hour and from day to day. Keep me from worrying about tomorrow, remembering that "sufficient unto the day is the evil thereof."

Give me peaceful days and restful nights. Bless me with sleep. Grant me health in body, soul, and mind. Comfort my soul with the promises of Thy Word, and keep me steadfast in the faith to the end. Make me grateful to those who are caring for me. Bless this household, and keep all of us cheerful, hopeful, and confident, trusting in Thee to do all things well. I ask this of Thee, who hast redeemed me with Thine own blood. Amen.

*Prayers During the Convalescent Period*

1

Gracious Father in heaven, Thy hand has been heavy on me, and the days of my illness have been trying. I thank Thee for the chastening, for through it Thou hast drawn me closer to Thee, and through it I have learned more than ever to realize that Thou art my loving Father. I pray Thee, forgive my fears and impatience during my severe trial, and forgive also the bad moments which I have caused those who lovingly cared for me. Remember no more any ingratitude which I may have shown.

I am now on the road to recovery. Lord, help me therefore to praise Thee every day and to remember Thy goodness and mercy. In the pain and difficult moments which still lie ahead, help me to think of the sufferings of Jesus Christ for my salvation; when I become impatient, help me to think of Thy patience with sinful man; when I fear for my salvation, help me to remember that my faith is preserved by the power of the Holy Spirit and not by anything that I can do.

Make me humbly grateful for every blessing which Thou hast given. Make the time of my convalescence pass quickly, and restore me to useful service if it please Thee to do so. Open ways for me to show my gratitude to Thee and to those who have served me in my illness, and finally bring me and all who are near and dear to me into Thy glorious presence, where sickness and sorrow will be no more; through Jesus Christ. Amen.

## 2

Heavenly Father, by Thy goodness I am recovering from serious illness. I was sick unto death, but Thou hast mercifully answered the prayers which were made for my recovery. I am indebted to Thee for the healing of my sick body.

"Bless the Lord, O my soul; and all that is within me, bless His holy name. Bless the Lord, O my soul, and forget not all His benefits, who forgiveth all thine iniquities, who healeth all thy diseases, who redeemeth thy life from destruction, who crowneth thee with loving-kindness and tender mercies."

For the period of convalescence grant me the grace to resign myself to Thy holy will. Help me to be patient when complete recovery is slow in coming. Open my eyes to see how Thou dost make all things, even my sickness and weakness, work together for my good. May Thy peace, which passeth all human understanding, fill my heart and mind.

In Jesus' glorious name. Amen.

3

Heavenly Father, Thou hast told Thy children to pray confidently in the name of Thy dear Son. Thou hast assured all that trust in Thee that Thou dost never weary of the pleas of Thy children, nor dost Thou turn a deaf ear to their petitions.

Because Thou hast invited me to Thy throne of grace, I ask Thee, if it be Thy will, to continue to bless my recovery and to restore me to healthful and helpful activity once more. Thanks be to Thee for having favored me with healing thus far and for having blessed the ministrations of the physician and others who have cared for me.

Give me a humble dependence on Thy gracious will, and keep me from becoming impatient, fretful, and distressing to myself and others. Grant me the grace to understand that this affliction is Thy means to a good end for me. Purify my faith during these days so that I gain a keener sense of values, a better understanding of Thy goodness, and a deeper appreciation of the blessings which surround me.

Thou wilt not fail me nor forsake me. In Thee do I hope all the day long. Amen.

# 4

Almighty and all-wise Father, I have been sick, and Thou art making me well. For Thy assistance on the road to recovery I give Thee humble thanks. I know Thou canst make me completely well if it be Thy will. Thou who commandest the sun and the stars canst also bid my sickness leave. The doctors and nurses are Thy instruments; but Thou dost bless, and Thou dost heal.

I desire so much to be restored to health that I may again perform my duties and participate in the activities I enjoy. I prefer to be helpful to others rather than to have others wait on me. If Thou wilt make me well again, I shall praise and glorify Thee by serving others all the days of my life.

However, if the road to recovery be long and painful, hold me by Thy loving hand, so that I may always feel Thee near me. Make me cheerful, considerate, and appreciative of kindnesses received. Above all, forgive me my sins through the blood of Jesus Christ, and make me holy in Thy sight. Give me that peace which the world cannot give. And when I reach journey's end, take me with Thee to heaven, where there is fullness of joy and where pain and sorrow are no more. Grant these requests for Jesus' sake. Amen.

During these days of recovery, gracious Lord, keep me calm and relaxed, unworried and untroubled. Let me always be mindful of Thy love, for Thou art the eternal Caretaker of the souls of mankind and art also thinking of me. In Thy wisdom and goodness direct my life that I may know each hour Thou art mindful of my welfare. I thank Thee and praise Thy precious name day after day. Let Thy healing hand hasten the day of my recovery, and help me to wait patiently on Thee without complaint. Bless those who take care of me. Grant that they perform their tasks cheerfully. Watch over all the sick, and draw them nearer with Thy healing grace through Jesus Christ, my Friend and Savior. Amen.

*At the Approach of Death*

Lord Jesus Christ, Thou Good Shepherd, I pray Thee to be with me in the hour of death. Let me feel even now the comfort and the assurance of Thy presence. Give me the faith to say: "Yea, though I walk through the valley of the shadow of death, I will fear no evil, for Thou art with me; Thy rod and Thy staff, they comfort me."

Comfort me with the assurance that Thou hast redeemed me from all sin, from death, and from the power of the devil and that I am Thine whether I live or whether I die.

Enable me in the face of death firmly to believe that Thy glorious resurrection from the dead has brought life and immortality to light. Give me the blessed hope that in Thee all shall be made alive, and that I, too, shall live again. "O Death, where is thy sting? O Grave, where is thy victory? . . . Thanks be to God, which giveth us the victory through our Lord Jesus Christ."

May Thy Holy Spirit preserve me in this faith until I reach the heavenly land. Amen, Lord Jesus, Amen.


*After a Death in the Family*

Heavenly Father, the death of my dear _____ has filled my eyes with tears and my heart with sorrow. I am distressed by the mysteries of Thy providence. As Thy child I want so much to say, "Not my will, but Thine be done," but at times I find it difficult to do. Forgive me and help me, I pray Thee, by Thy Holy Spirit, to accept Thy ways as always best.

Apply to my wounded heart the balm of Thy precious promises, and let me soon experience its healing power. Teach me not to mourn as those who have no hope. Wipe away the tears from my eyes that I may be able to see through the mist, beyond death and grave, to the resurrection and life assured by the glorious victory of my Savior Jesus Christ over death and grave.

May the passing of my _____ remind me that I, too, am but a pilgrim and stranger on earth. Grant me grace to love less and less the things which are material and temporal, and to love more and more the things which are spiritual and eternal. Teach me to number my days and to apply my heart to the wisdom taught by Jesus Christ, that He is the Way and the Truth and the Life, and that no man cometh unto Thee but by Him. Amen.

*For the Sorrowing*

O Father of mercies and God of all comfort, look down upon me in my sorrow and affliction. Comfort me with Thy gracious consolations. As an earthly father pities his children, have compassion on me in my suffering. May the loss I have suffered be for me a token of Thy love. In my distress lift me up to Thee. Remind me that in Thy mysterious providence all things work together for good to them that love Thee. Thou hast ordained that I together with all believers must through much tribulation enter into Thy kingdom.

May the fiery furnace of affliction, into which Thou hast cast me, by the mercies of Christ refine my heart from the dross of sin and help me to emerge a stronger Christian, better equipped to understand the problems and to deal with the troubles of others. Cause the loss which I have suffered to remind me that the things of earth are as a shadow which continueth not, that I may be inclined to set my affections on things above and not on things on earth. But above all, grant me the sure conviction that Thy will and Thy ways are best; through Jesus Christ, our Lord. Amen.

*Intercessions for the Sick*

O God of mercy and of might, with whom nothing is impossible, and whose delight is to come to the aid of the afflicted and distressed, show Thyself the very present Help in the sickness which has befallen ———. Comfort him (her) with the blessed assurance of the forgiveness of his (her) sins and grant him (her) patience in suffering until in Thy wisdom and gracious providence he (she) may be restored to health again, that the glory of his (her) restoration may be Thine and we all may praise and magnify Thy power and love, through Jesus Christ, our Savior. Amen.

Almighty and most merciful God, Thou great Physician, we come before Thee with a prayer in behalf of ———, who lies in dire need of help.

Thou knowest the pain, the danger, and the temptations which have beset him (her), and Thou alone canst provide the relief and help which will perfectly answer the needs that here present themselves. We beseech Thee with full confidence in Thy love and power that Thou mayest graciously behold, visit, and relieve Thy distressed child and grant him (her) the joy of praising Thee for his (her) deliverance. Teach us all to value health and strength as a precious gift from Thee, and help us to join in thanksgiving for all the healing Thou dost daily provide in our bodies and souls, through Jesus Christ, our Lord. Amen.

Almighty, everlasting God, the eternal Salvation of them that believe, hear our prayers in behalf of Thy servants who are sick, for whom we implore the aid of Thy mercy. Graciously heal their bodies and refresh their souls with Thy comfort, that, being restored to health, they may render thanks to Thee in Thy church; through Jesus Christ, Thy Son, our Lord. Amen.

*Table Prayers*

*Grace at Meals*

### 1

At this table be our Host,
Father, Son, and Holy Ghost!
Food and drink are from above,
Tokens of Thy heavenly love.
    Amen.

### 2

Lord God, our heavenly Father, bless this food which Thou hast given. Cause it to nourish my body that I may be able the better to serve Thee and those about me; for Jesus' sake. Amen.

### 3

Heavenly Father, with sincere appreciation we accept these gifts coming from Thy bountiful hand and gracious heart. Grant that we be grateful at all times for Thy benedictions and blessings, for Jesus' sake. Amen.

## 4

Lord, Thou Giver of all that is good, we thank Thee for the bountiful meal which is spread before us. We acknowledge this food as a gift of Thy love and as an invitation to bring our needs and our thanks to Thee. Bless the food which Thou hast given. Grant us the grace to receive it as an undeserved blessing from Thee, and nourish our bodies thereby, that we may be enabled to serve Thee the more; in the name of Jesus. Amen.

## 5

We ask Thee, Lord Jesus, to honor us with Thy presence at our meal. Thou hast graciously provided the food we are about to eat and hast given us the health to enjoy Thy blessings. Sanctify our hearts to receive Thy blessings to our profit and to Thy great joy. Amen.

*Prayers of Thanks*

## 1

Heavenly Father,
> For these blessings from Thy store
> Keep me thankful evermore. Amen.

## 2

Dear Father in heaven, we thank Thee for the food we eat. We thank Thee for the friends we meet. We thank Thee for Thy loving care. In Jesus' name we thank Thee. Amen.

## 3

We give thanks to Thee, gracious Father in Christ Jesus, for the food which Thou hast provided for us in Thy goodness and love. Grant that at all times we recognize Thy lovingkindness toward us and show our sincere appreciation of all that we have received. We say thanks in Jesus' name. Amen.

## 4

Dear Father in heaven, we thank Thee for the refreshment of body and mind which has come to us through the food which Thou hast given. Make us ever thankful for all gifts of Thy mercy, and make us faithful in their use. Show us how best to serve Thee, and give us the willingness to spend our lives in thankful service to Thee; in the name of Jesus. Amen.

## 5

We thank Thee, Lord God, heavenly Father, for Thy faithful providence which we have enjoyed and for Thy gracious provision of fellowship with one another and with Thee. Teach us to receive Thy gifts with thanksgiving, that with grateful hearts we may enjoy the gifts which have come from Thee, who together with the Son and the Holy Ghost art one God and one Lord. Amen.

*The Benedictions of the Lord*

*The Old Testament Benediction*

The Lord bless thee and keep thee; the Lord make His face shine upon thee and be gracious unto thee; the Lord lift up His countenance upon thee and give thee peace. Numbers 6:24-26.

*The New Testament Benedictions*

The grace of the Lord Jesus Christ and the love of God and the communion of the Holy Ghost be with you all. 2 Corinthians 13:14.

The grace of our Lord Jesus Christ be with you all. Now to Him that is of power to stablish you according to my Gospel, and the preaching of Jesus Christ, according to the revelation of the mystery which was kept secret since the world began but now is made manifest, and by the Scriptures of the prophets, according to the commandment of the everlasting God, made known to all nations for the obedience of faith — to God only wise, be glory through Jesus Christ forever. Romans 16:24-27.

Peace be to the brethren, and love with faith, from God the Father and the Lord Jesus Christ. Grace be with all them that love our Lord Jesus Christ in sincerity. Ephesians 6:23, 24.

Now the Lord of peace Himself give you peace always by all means. The Lord be with you all. The grace of our Lord Jesus Christ be with you all. 2 Thessalonians 3:16, 18.

The Lord Jesus Christ be with thy spirit. Grace be with you. 2 Timothy 4:22.

Now the God of peace that brought again from the dead our Lord Jesus, that Great Shepherd of the sheep, through the blood of the everlasting covenant, make you perfect in every good work to do His will, working in you that which is well-pleasing in His sight, through Jesus Christ, to whom be glory forever and ever. Hebrews 13:20, 21.

Grow in grace and in the knowledge of our Lord and Savior Jesus Christ. To Him be glory both now and forever. 2 Peter 3:18.

Now unto Him that is able to keep you from falling and to present you faultless before the presence of His glory with exceeding joy, to the only wise God, our Savior, be glory and majesty, dominion and power, both now and ever. Amen. Jude 24, 25.

Now the God of hope fill you with all joy and peace in believing, that ye may abound in hope, through the power of the Holy Ghost. Romans 15:13.

Now unto Him that is able to do exceeding abundantly above all that we ask or think, according to the power that worketh in us, unto Him be glory in the church by Christ Jesus throughout all ages, world without end. Ephesians 3:20, 21.

Now unto the King eternal, immortal, invisible, the only wise God, be honor and glory forever and ever. 1 Timothy 1:17.

But the God of all grace, who hath called us unto His eternal glory by Christ Jesus, after that ye have suffered a while, make you perfect, stablish, strengthen, settle you. To Him be glory and dominion forever and ever. 1 Peter 5:10, 11.

Blessing and glory and wisdom and thanksgiving and honor and power and might be unto our God forever and ever. Revelation 7:12.

# WHERE TO FIND IT IN THE BIBLE

The Ten Commandments —
   Exodus 20 and Deuteronomy 5
The Lord's Prayer — Matthew 6 and Luke 11
The Beatitudes — Matthew 5
The Parable of the Good Samaritan — Luke 10
The Parable of the Prodigal Son — Luke 15
The Seven Letters of Jesus — Revelation 2 and 3
The Sermon on the Mount — Matthew 5—7
The Seven Words from the Cross —
   Matthew 27; Luke 23; John 19
The Pentecost Account — Acts 2
The Fruits of the Spirit — Galatians 5:22-26
The Penitential Psalms —
   Psalms 6; 32; 38; 51; 102; 130; 143
The Psalm of Moses — Psalm 90
The Lord's Supper —
   Matthew 26; Mark 14; Luke 22; 1 Corinthians 11
The Institution of Baptism — Matthew 28:19, 20
The Sum Total of the Gospel — John 3:16
Salvation Through the Blood of Christ —
   Romans 3:20-28
Tables of Duties: For Children, Ephesians 6:1-3; for Fathers, Ephesians 6:4; for Husbands, Ephesians 5:25-33; for Wives, Ephesians 5:22-24; for Employers, Ephesians 6:9; for Employees, Ephesians 6:5-8; for Citizens, Romans 13 and 1 Peter 2:13-17.

# OUTSTANDING STORIES IN THE BIBLE

The Life of Abraham — Genesis 12—25:10
The Story of Jacob and Rachel — Genesis 29
The Life of Joseph — Genesis 37—50
The Birth and Call of Moses — Exodus 2 and 3
The Story of Balaam and Balak — Numbers 22—24
The Fall of Jericho — Joshua 6
The Conquests of Gideon — Judges 6—8
The Strange Ways of Samson — Judges 13—16
The Story of Ruth — The Book of Ruth
David, the Shepherd Boy — 1 Samuel 16 and 17
The Friendship of David and Jonathan — 1 Samuel 18 to 20
Elijah the Tishbite — 1 Kings 17—21 and 2 Kings 2
The Cleansing of Naaman, the Leper — 2 Kings 5
Queen Esther — The Book of Esther
Daniel and His Friends — Daniel 1—6
King Hezekiah — Isaiah 36—39
Jonah and the Great Fish — The Book of Jonah
Job and His Misfortunes — Job 1, 2, 42
The Life of Jesus According to Luke
The Man Born Blind — John 9
The Footwashing in the Upper Room — John 13
Peter and John at the Gate Beautiful — Acts 3
The Shipwreck of Paul — Acts 27 and 28

## OUTSTANDING CHAPTERS OF THE OLD TESTAMENT

Genesis 1
Numbers 35
Deuteronomy 28
Joshua 1
1 Samuel 3
2 Samuel 12
2 Kings 7
2 Chronicles 6
Job 14
Job 19
Job 38
Proverbs 30

Proverbs 31
Isaiah 6
Isaiah 40
Isaiah 44
Isaiah 53
Isaiah 61
Ezekiel 3
Ezekiel 37
Ezekiel 47
Joel 2
Malachi 3

*Favorite Psalms*

Psalms 2; 19; 23; 24; 27; 37; 42; 46; 51; 63; 84; 90; 91; 100; 103; 118; 121; 139

## OUTSTANDING CHAPTERS OF THE NEW TESTAMENT

Matthew 11
Matthew 13
Mark 10
Luke 2
Luke 7
Luke 15
Luke 16
Luke 18
Luke 24
John 3
John 4
John 10
John 11
John 14
John 15

Acts 8
Acts 10
Acts 26
Romans 5
Romans 8
1 Corinthians 13
1 Corinthians 15
Galatians 6
Ephesians 2
Ephesians 5
Philippians 4
Hebrews 11
James 3
1 Peter 1
Revelation 3